THE CATHOLIC UNIVERSITY C

PHILOSOPHICAL STUDIE

Volume 184

Abstract No. 35

Material and Formal Causality in the Philosophy of Aristotle and St. Thomas

AN ABSTRACT OF A DISSERTATION

SUBMITTED TO THE FACULTY OF THE SCHOOL OF PHILOSOPHY
OF THE CATHOLIC UNIVERSITY OF AMERICA IN PARTIAL
FULFILLMENT OF THE REQUIREMENTS FOR THE
DEGREE OF DOCTOR OF PHILOSOPHY

BY

REV. LAWRENCE F. LYONS, S. S. E., M. A.

THE CATHOLIC UNIVERSITY OF AMERICA PRESS
WASHINGTON, D. C.

1958

Imprimi potest:

Very Reverend J. T. PURTILL, S. S. E.
Superior General

Nihil obstat:

Right Reverend CHARLES A. HART
Censor Deputatus

Imprimatur:

✠ Most Reverend PATRICK A. O'BOYLE
Archbishop of Washington

May 14, 1958.

PRINTED IN THE UNITED STATES OF AMERICA
BY J. H. FURST COMPANY, BALTIMORE, MARYLAND

PREFACE

The writing of the preface of a doctoral dissertation is perhaps the most pleasant aspect of graduate study. The preface is at once an indication of the completion of the work and an opportunity for expression of the writer's gratitude both to those who made the course of study possible and to those who actively aided in the completion of the work.

The writer is indebted to the Society of Saint Edmund and to his Superiors for the opportunity to pursue four years of graduate study. He is happy to acknowledge a friendly, scholarly and priestly association with the Very Reverend Ignatius Smith, O. P., the late Dean of the School of Philosophy, and with his successor, the Right Reverend Monsignor John K. Ryan, whose scholarly direction and encouragement is deeply appreciated.

To Right Reverend Monsignor Charles A. Hart the writer owes his greatest debt of gratitude for the original inspiration and the patient and helpful direction of the dissertation. His years of study at *The Catholic University of America* will ever be remembered for this a pleasant and profitable association with Monsignor Hart in his dual role of priest and Christian philosopher.

The writer is especially grateful to Reverend Doctor George Reilly and Doctor Roy Bode for their careful reading of and critical commentary upon the manuscript.

TABLE OF CONTENTS

INTRODUCTION

E. I. Watkin some time ago published an interesting book on *The Philosophy of Form*.[1] Long before the time of Watkin, Clemens Baeumker wrote on the Problem of Matter.[2] It might be supposed that one was taking advantage of a fortunate bibliographical situation in proposing a single work on the two notions considered as comprising one philosophical principle. Yet, therein lies the seed of inspiration for, and the justification of, this thesis. I do not propose to write a philosophy of form as form, nor even of matter as matter. I propose a study of both form and matter, taken as one and mutually and reciprocally causative, in relation to the being of the existents of which they are principles.

To say by way of introduction that causality or causation is the viewpoint or formal object of this essay, is not to say enough. Aristotle left the generic notion strangely undefined. For St. Thomas Aquinas, whose writings will provide the source material for much of this work, cause is defined existentially. To be a cause is to contribute in any or all of four ways to the being (existence) of a thing. The ultimate concern here will be neither matter, nor form, nor cause, but being as being, an essence, exercising the act of to be.

This is not a pioneer effort in the treatment of cause. Others [3] have prepared the way for this thesis by showing that being by its very structure demands the existence of causes, extrinsic causes. Such a preparation was necessary. For, if there is no place in reality for causation, the question as to the existence of material and formal causes need not be raised. That which has no efficient cause cannot have a material cause. This indicates that the basic significance of material and formal causality must be found in

---

[1] E. I. Watkin, *The Philosophy of Form*.
[2] C. Baeumker, *Das Problem der Materie in der Griechischen Philosophie*.
[3] F. Meehan, *Efficient Causality in Aristotle and St. Thomas*; R. J. Collins, "The Metaphysical Basis of Finality in St. Thomas."

their relation to the act of existence which is the effect of the operation of an efficient cause. True, matter is in potency to receive the actuality that is its form, but the union of form and matter must first be brought about by the action of efficient causes acting purposively. Matter and form are the constitutive principles of the material being, but the efficient cause is the first cause of that material being.

This study is not an attempt at complete treatment of the philosophical problem of material being. That is matter for the philosophy of nature. Our primary concern is the problem of individuation of material being, considered both as a consequence of the problem of individuality in being and as a contributing factor in our explanation of the structure of material being. How does the mutual and reciprocal causality of matter and form contribute to a satisfactory explanation of being as being understood in existential terms?

The problems which are involved here have their roots in the past but their consequences frequently are solved only in the future. Such is the problem of individuality and individuation. There is permanence and yet there is change which is more than accidental. These are the two factors which give rise to the problem which the early Greeks proposed, Plato and Aristotle attempted to solve and St. Thomas Aquinas resolved. It is a real and pressing problem. Men are aware of the existence of individual beings which manifest similarity of nature with other existents of a class. How is this similarity to be explained? This is the so-called problem of individuation, as distinguished from the prior problem of the individuality of beings where class membership is not the immediate problem. Individuality comes face to face with Parmenides and seeks to explain the distinction of each existing being from every other being in the universe. Insofar as this problem was solved at all in antiquity, the problem of individuality was best solved by Aristotle; for a failure to recognize this problem is symptomatic of a tendency to confuse and equate it with that of individuation. From our vantage point in history, we can say (although Aristotle would undoubtedly object strenuously to our oversimplification), that the Stagirite's solution was solely on the basis of individuation. As a philosophical position, individuality, on the other hand, is purely Thomistic. St. Thomas locates the principle of difference within the individual essence, each individual possessing to some degree the perfections of its class. The principle of limitation is here potential essence, or prime matter. The actual essence, so limited, is called substantial form and as received into the matter, it becomes a distinct individual material substance; it is individuated.

The use of hylomorphism to explain rationally the existence of many distinct individuals of a single class, is peculiarly Thomistic. It bears only nominal similarity to its original formulation by Aristotle who used the theory in a purely physical context to explain substantial or essential change. Thomistic hylomorphism is immediately metaphysical because it is existential; it is intimately related to individual acts of existence rather than to mere forms of existence. We hope to indicate that it is only this more ultimate relation of matter and form to act of existence that validates the claim of hylomorphism to be a metaphysical explanation of the structure of real essences of material substances, and justifies its use in the philosophy of nature as an explanation of physical change.

Turning back the pages of history one gradually becomes aware that St. Thomas Aquinas made of the philosophy of Aristotle something rather different from historic Aristotelianism. The Greek philosopher was concerned with the problem of motion, in the wide sense of becoming, whereas Aquinas made the problem of existence the primary metaphysical concern of his philosophy. The former asked what things are and how they come to be what they are, but he did not raise the question of why they exist at all; of why there is something rather than nothing. There is a very great deal of difference between the two questions.

The two problems cannot, indeed, be dissociated from one another, for they are but two aspects of the same metaphysical problem of participation. If we call the first the " essentialist aspect,' and the second the ' existentialist aspect,' it is precisely because in this existential aspect of his philosophy that Aquinas goes beyond Aristotle. The Stagirite did not raise the problem of the existence of finite things. In fact he did not realize that there is a problem, because he concentrated on what a thing is, that is, on the ways in which a thing is or can be, rather than on its act of existence. The Angelic Doctor, however, while retaining the

Aristotelian metaphysics of substance and accident, form and matter, act and potency, emphasized in his own metaphysics not essence, not *what* a thing is, but the very existence of the essence considered as the act of existing. This change of emphasis significantly altered the Angelic Doctor's metaphysical inheritance from Aristotle. Although, for Aristotle, finite substances exist, they are analyzed solely in terms of their changing forms with no reference to their *dependence* for existence. The world of Aristotle is a world of substances, but it is eternal and uncreated. It is against this background that he defined his notion of substance. St. Thomas adopted the Aristotelian analysis and adapted it to a world of finite substances, each of which is totally dependent upon God. The Saint does not intrinsically alter the analysis of the nature of substance; but rather significantly enlarges the understanding of substance in the light of revelation. All material substances change. St. Thomas, as well as Aristotle, held that in every material thing there are two distinguishable principles, the substantial form and the prime matter. In accordance with Aristotle's entelechy, form is the determining immanent constitutive principle of activity. Form stamps a purely potential and indeterminate prime matter as *this* particular type of organism, determining it to act in certain *specified* ways.

Superficial investigation of the problem of individuation frequently has led to the precipitant conclusion that Aquinas merely borrowed from Aristotle. More careful consideration shows that this is not the case. It is to be hoped that the conclusions reached in this thesis will provide a deterrent to ill-advised zeal indiscriminately to label 'Aristotelian' any one facet of Thomism. The terminology used by St. Thomas is often the same as that used by the Philosopher, but on the part of Aristotle all is subordinated to form, and on the part of Aquinas to act of existence. This seems to bring the Stagerite closer to his master Plato, than St. Thomas to Aristotle. For Aristotle, as well as for Plato, not only was the universal essence the only subject of true knowledge, but in Aristotle it was ultimately identical with the real essence in the individual. The form is one in Aristotle and it is one in Plato. But in Plato the individual was merely a transitory phenomenal manifestation of an Idea (Form), which was the true reality. Aristotelian form received into matter as many times as the number of given individual things demands, implies no limitation of essence. The same form exists in many given parts of changeable and indivisible matter. Again, only the form is real in the full sense of the word. The form is not changed, not limited, but merely received in many different matters. The consequences are tremendous in scope; they permeate every phase of being. The individual is lost in the class; author and critic are lost in humanity. History, written in the genre of a Durkheim and a Comte becomes meaningful; the individual is lost in society.

Aristotle identified being with essence or substance. He nowhere considers the distinct act of to be as a co-principle of being received into essence as into a limiting principle. But according to Aquinas every material thing is composed of substantial form and prime matter. Neither of these principles of itself is a thing. The two together are components or parts of the one essence which in turn is potential to existence. Since Aristotle did not consider the act of *to be* as a distinct principle of the thing, he could not clearly distinguish individual existences within a given class of similar essences.

The problem which Parmenides raised has ever remained the first problem of philosophy. As beings are prior to species, so individuality as a problem is prior to individuation. The existence of the individual among the manifold of the universe must be explained if any philosophy is to stand upon a rational foundation. Justification of individual existences must be prior to any thought of the preservation of the reality of individuals within the species. As being is prior to species and individuality to individuation, so the problem of limitation and multiplication of existing beings is necessarily prior to limitation and multiplication in the order of essences. If Aristotle's solution of the latter problem is incomplete, it is because he overlooked the former problem. The solution does not lie in any exaggerated formalism, which pretends to find in reality an exact replica of the logical structure of abstract knowledge. It rests rather on the real structure of being, demanding a dual source to insure complete reality of every individual in a specific order. St. Thomas' solution of the problem of the twofold limitation of material beings is grounded upon a determined conception of hylomorphism; the matter is pure potency, the substantial form of every individual is *unique*. Matter and form are essentially correlatives, and the hylomorphic structure is real only by reason of a principle of existence distinct from this structure.

This thesis attempts to show how the philosophy of a mediaeval monk molded hylomorphism into a coherent account of how many beings preserve distinction in class membership (individuation), and distinction in existence (individuality). The Dominican philosopher used potency and act, as did Aristotle before him, to explain substantial change. For both Aristotle and Aquinas matter indicates capacity for determination, a certain moreness of form or essence. In addition, for St. Thomas alone, the essence indicates a limitation to this much and no more essence.

Being and becoming, individuality and individuation, substantial existence and substantial change were the problems that faced St. Thomas Aquinas. They are the problems which must be considered in this thesis, with the specific intention of evaluating the effect which his solution of them had upon his metaphysics. We speak of one thing becoming another, implying thereby that there is both continuity and discontinuity in change. Continuity, because that which changes is not annihilated; discontinuity, because there is first one and then another *kind* of thing. We speak of this determination of the determinable in terms of matter and form—the hylomorphic theory—which at first sight seems a physical theory to explain substantial change. More careful consideration, however, seems to indicate a purely metaphysical theory; hylomorphism is but another phase of essence and existence. Prime matter is not, and indeed cannot be, the direct object of experience; it is postulated as the result of an analysis of experience, and this analysis is obviously not the physical or chemical analysis of contemporary positive science. The language of the theory belongs to metaphysics and not to science. Aquinas regarded the hylomorphic theory as being independent of contemporary ideas about such physical elements as fire and water, and as being the result of metaphysical rather than physical experience. It involves a metaphysical reasoning. We cannot see either matter or form, but we reason to the former from substantial change, and to the latter from the characteristic activities of the organism.

If the theory of matter and form is interpreted as a metaphysical theory and as being independent of the results of empirical scientific research, it follows that no new empirically verifiable

scientific propositions can be derived from it. We may deduce from
the theory the possibility of changes of a certain type. Observation
of these changes is, however, the principal basis for the original
assertion of the theory and, therefore, the conclusion as to the possibility of such changes would not be a new empirically verifiable
proposition. Hence the theory cannot be used as an instrument in
the progress of natural science. Father Copleston states that " for
the purpose of natural science the theory is ' useless,' if by a theory's
being ' useful ' in natural science one means that new empirically
verifiable, or rather testable, propositions can be derived from it." [4]
Hylomorphism has, however, a contribution to make to physical
science. By presenting a world which is not simply and solely a
Heraclitean flux, but shot through with intelligibility, hylomorphism maintains itself as a preparatory condition for, and stimulus
to, empirical scientific research, for the reason that reflection upon
the activity of reality provides some knowledge of its intelligible
structure.

If we insist upon the truth of hylomorphism with respect to the
scientific theories of the atomic structure of material things, we
must insist upon its metaphysical character even more, for this
character establishes its independence of any and all of the changing hypotheses of science. Matter and form, in relation to act of
existence, are the metaphysical constitutive principles of bodies, in
the sense that reflective analysis of bodies or of corporeal substance
as such, rather than this or that kind of corporeality, reveals their
presence. The theory may be useless in the sense indicated above by
Father Copleston, but to say this is simply to say that the theory
is not a theory of empirical science. From the writings of St.
Thomas we shall show that the Angelic Doctor regarded the theory
as being prior to empirical scientific research, just as metaphysics
has at least a priority of nature to physics. Showing, from his
writings, that this is the mind of St. Thomas will involve us in
an evaluation of both the Platonic and Aristotelian elements of
Thomistic thought.

Plato and Aristotle are two of the greatest philosophers the world
has even seen. Frequent similarities of thought often fail to con-
ceal a marked difference of outlook between them. If one prescinds

[4] F. Copleston, *Aquinas*, p. 88.

from those not inconsiderable elements common to both of them, one might, to borrow Hegelian terminology, characterize their respective philosophies as standing to one another in the relation of thesis (Platonism) to antithesis (Aristotelianism); a thesis and antithesis which demand reconcilation in a higher synthesis.

St. Thomas Aquinas provided this synthesis which is a synthesis of the ideal and the real. His consideration of the real in terms of the ideal provided a coherent statement of the transcendental principles of being. From his experience of the individual as limited, material and finite, the Angelic Doctor rose to an elaboration of the principles and laws of being *qua* being—principles that explained the very individuality of the beings from which he obtained his original data. His notion of being permeated every question and gave meaning to every facet of his philosophy. His every thought and action were directed towards a deeper penetration of being, an attempt to relate each thing to its own act of existing and all things to the utlimate act of existence which is God. That was his task. Ours shall be to show how his doctrine of material and formal causality, in contrast to that of Aristotle, becomes more comprehensive when viewed in relation to his notion of being as act of existing.

This dissertation originally envisioned five parts: Matter and Form in relation to the act of existence in (1) Pre-Socratic and Platonic Philosophy, (2) In Aristotle, (3) In Neoplatonic and Augustinian Thought, (4) In St. Thomas Aquinas, and (5) In Modern Philosophy of Science. Considerations of time and space eliminated part three. It was considered sufficient for the purpose of this dissertation merely to indicate the origin of the Platonic theory of ideas which in some way may have influenced St. Thomas' notion of participation in being. The Neoplatonic theory of participation as an influence upon Thomism, especially through St. Augustine, is in itself matter for a doctoral dissertation. 'The vast scope of research in contemporary physical science indicates that part five is in itself matter for the doctoral dissertation of a student who is both a philosopher and scientist. We should have liked to discuss matter and form in the Neoplatonic commentators and St. Augustine as a connecting link in the history of philosophy between the ancient and mediaeval notions of material and formal causality. Again, however, temporal and spatial considerations rendered impractical the composition of material gathered on this interesting phase of the history of matter and form.

The present work is more cohesive in design and realistic in content. The purpose of this thesis is to present, contrast and evaluate the replies of Plato, Aristotle, and St. Thomas Aquinas to dilemma of Parmenides. The work treats of being, matter and form to the extent that these elements give rise to, and present a possibility for, a solution of the dual problem of Individuality and Individuation. The thesis consists of three parts: (I) Matter and Form in Pre-Socratic and Platonic Philosophy, (II) Matter and Form in Aristotle's Thought, and (III) The Significance of Material and Formal Causality in the thought of St. Thomas Aquinas. Within these dimensions are presented the Pre-Socratic and Platonic origins of the notions of matter and form; Aristotle's development of these notions in terms of material and formal causes; and finally, the significance attached to material and formal causality by St. Thomas who related these and all the causes to the act of existence.

Part I lays the foundation for the comparative studies which comprise Parts II and III. In Part I the notions of matter and form and causality are discovered. These notions, together with the notion of being which they manifest, will provide some of the basic material of this thesis. The theory of causality is the best indication of the notion of being advanced by any given philosophical system. For this reason both Part II and Part III treat in detail the respective theories of causality of Aristotle and St. Thomas for the light they can shed upon the notion of being peculiar to each. Matter and form are fashioned by the Stagirite into a theory of causality which sublimates all the causes to the formal cause. The formal cause as the act of essence is identified with being. Form is that which gives being and meaning to all that is. In fact, it may be considered as that formal aspect which gives unity and coherence to all of Arisotle's philosophy.

Part III presents the views of Thomism, both mediaeval and modern, on material and formal causality. In so doing it presents a justification for the title and a solution of the problems presented in this dissertation. As the notion of form predominated Part II, the notion of existence (*esse*) dominates Part III. For what form is to historical Aristotelianism, *esse* is to Thomism both mediaeval and modern. St. Thomas Aquinas also considered being as an act, but as act of existence. He presents a theory of causality in which all causes influence the act of being. Matter and form take on added significance; they contribute positively to the being of a thing. But as essence is subordinated to existence, so are matter and form subordinated to the act of existence. Form as the act of essence, ever remains potential to existence. Matter and form as act and potency provide a metaphysical explanation to individuation, but as species are posterior to being, so hylomorphism is secondary to the distinction of essence and existence. Material and formal causality provide a satisfactory explanation of individuation but only as this problem is consequential to that of individuality. The two applications of act and potency, individuality and individuation are almost as correlative as act and potency themselves, but as act must always be prior to potentiality, so matter and form must be subject to *esse*, as individuality is to individuation and metaphysics to physics.

Although the material becomes progressively more theoretical, the method, in keeping with the original inspiration of this thesis and the developmental character of human thought, remains historical throughout. In fact, if being and hylomorphism considered in terms of individuality and individuation are the matter, historical method might be considered as the form of this dissertation. The work is not intended to be a study in history as history, but an investigation of the body of historical fact in an effort to contribute to the scope of philosophical experience.

CHAPTER I

MATTER AND FORM IN PRE-SOCRATIC PHILOSOPHY

The History of Philosophy from Thales to the present is dominated by the attempt to explain reality in terms of the concepts of matter and form. Such an history is but a chronicle of man's ascent from the order of things (beings) to the realm of Being Itself; from the observation of things that are, to the study of all that is, precisely as it is. Philosophers have always searched for an explanation of the reality that they experienced. Both science and philosophy shared in their intellectual evolution. Insofar as they went beyond simple organization of a body of facts and attempted to set forth reason for such organization, they were indeed philosophers. Consequently, our concern with them here, is a philosophical one, or more properly, a cosmological one. Whether or not, and to what extent their attempt may be considered as a search for the causes of things, and of profit to a more complete explanation of reality, will be the burden of this chapter.

Certain conclusions may be drawn from the search of Greek Philosophy for material and formal causes. First: the problem that the Greeks faced was the problem of change; a change of being from one thing into another thing. It was a question of the nature or essence of things, not existence; for, they assumed that everything was of one fundamental nature. They attempted a solution of the problem of change by a search for the fundamental nature from which all things come and into which all return. These are but two aspects of the same problem, the perennial philosophical enigma of the One and/or the Many. The Greeks seemed to have grasped this point only gradually in their philosophical development as they progressed from the first two levels of thought to metaphysical thinking.

Secondly: the Greek concept of matter may be considered as causative, to this extent at least, that they considered various different kinds of matter as the *principle* from which all else proceeds. We speak thus, of matter as a cause in the broad sense of the meaning of Aristotle's ἡ αἰτία. That is, not only a being which exerts influence on another distinct from itself (an extrinsic cause), but with regard to matter as entering into the constitution of a being. Thus matter for the Greeks is in an intrinsic cause, which by entering into the constitution of the being plays a role in the manner of being which the thing enjoys. Thus it seems that in early Greek philosophy at least, that matter could be considered as being a constitutive principle without necessarily being causative in the strict sense of the term. This should not be understood as vitiating our statement to the effect that there was a material cause in Greek philosophy. The early Greeks contributed to the History of Philosophy the notion that matter was in some way causative. It remained to future generations of philosophers to complete this immature theory of etiology.[1]

The pre-Socratics was indeed philosophers. "They did not believe that anything *is* by chance." [2] We have seen that knowledge was the object of their inquiry and they did not consider they knew the thing until they had grasped the "why" of it.[3] Although the word cause (αἰτία) was not used by them, their extant reports indicate that they were seeking a material principle or source of material things. They were concerned with a material cause and motion; motion being an essential characteristic of all matter. Nothing could be generated or corrupted because matter is something out of which other things are formed and into which they are dissolved, but which, though changing its attributes, remains essentially the same. Later Ionians, like Empedocles and Anaxagoras, would see that the problem of the generation of things had been left unanswered by their predecessors.[4]

With Aristotle then, we may conclude that the Ionian etiology, if we may dignify their theory with the title, was concerned only with the material cause especially as it was seen to be the cause of motion. No inquiry was made into final and formal causes. Even their inquiry into material and efficient causes, was but a child-

---

[1] There does not seem to have been any real notion in Greek Philosophy of form as causative until the time of Plato. There is, however, some evidence for believing that the Pythogoreans had a notion of number as both a material principle and also as a principle of the formation of things.

[2] Aristotle, *Physics*, II, 4, 196a10 (Italics added).

[3] *Ibid.*, 3, 194b18-20.   [4] *Metaph.*, I, 3, 984a9.

ish stammer in the light of future refinements of etiology by Aristotle.[5]

For the Ionians motion was an essential characteristic of all matter. Nothing could be really generated or corrupted because matter is something out of which other things are formed and into which they are dissolved, but which, though changing its attributes, still remains essentially the same.

An occupational hazard of a study of the history of Ancient Philosophy is the danger, in discussing old thinkers, of reading into their thought, the intellectual refinements of a later age. Perfection of interpretation requires the mortification of this tendency so it is at odds with historical methodology. We must not overestimate their importance, nor yet denude them of significance in the words of two recent historians of science. " These philosophers are, according to the accurate title given to them in antiquity, *physiologi*, that is to say observers of nature. . . . They observe phenomena which present themselves to their eyes, and putting aside all supernatural or mystical intervention, they endeavor to give strictly natural explanations of them." [6]

To say this is not to say enough; for, they were not simple observers of nature. They were natural scientists whose eyes had been opened, whose attention directed, and whose observation of phenomena had been conditioned and quickened by a desire to know the causes of things. Since the fear of unexplained reality may be considered as the beginning of wisdom, and since the early Greeks attempted to provide additional explanation of reality, they are rightly considered the first philosophers. They are representative of the first level of abstractive thought, as the Pythagoreans are of the second or matematical level. It remained for Plato and Aristotle, in attempting to answer the Parmenidean dilemma to attain the heights of metaphysical thinking—the third level of human thought. In Plato's default it remained to Aristotle to provide the best Greek solution to our problem. We may suggest that since he too took up the problem in terms of the problem of substantial change, that he too remained on the level of thought peculiar to the Natural Philosopher.

[5] *Ibid.*, I, 10, 993a11-16.

[6] Brunet et Mieli, *Histoire des Sciences.* Antiquité, p. 114; as quoted by B. Farrington, *Greek Science*, p. 41.

Chapter II

THE SIGNIFICANCE OF PLATO'S THOUGHT

As to the significance of the Platonic period in the history of matter and form, we may conclude that the discovery of a philosophical formal cause was now a fact. The reality of a material cause in Plato's philosophy is a less valid conclusion. An explanation of change in terms of a being peculiar to the abstraction of a metaphysician accords Plato a revered place among philosophers, as one of the first metaphysicians. His notions of space and form as co-principles and factors contributing to the solution of becoming (even if only the original becoming), merit him lengthy mention. These same principles as the foundations of his theory of participation (if indeed his participation theory can be considered distinct from the original becoming) insure him of frequent mention in pages to come.

Plato momentarily had the answer to Parmenides' problem, but vitiated it when he identified being with space. Matter is that which receives the likeness of the ideas. Since ideas are that which is, matter must be that which is not, sort of a non-being. Plato's notion is also vitiated by its subsequent identification with space. Aristotle, in his notion of privation or non-being on the level of essences, purged the notion of its contradiction but did not speak in terms of existence. Both failed to answer Parmenides' problem as Parmenides himself posed it. Plato, however, did attempt to answer it. He recognized that non-being had to play a role in the overall solution. Perhaps Plato's individuation failed because of a prior failure to explain the individuality of each being; and this failure meant that he had not explained precisely how there are many beings. Believing that he was discussing the distinction of beings, Plato suggested how there could be many individuals in a class and St. Thomas will take this suggestion as the basis of his explanation of the same problem. Plato did not trace the Parmenidean problem in the realm of being as being but on the level

4

of the distinction of beings in a class; that is, the many under the one eternal idea. The individuals participate in some way in the being of the idea. Although not answering the question put to him, Plato did state clearly the Parmenidean problem in terms of a notion of a non-being that is not nothing. For this the history of philosophy is grateful. Plato suggested how there could be many individuals in a class. St. Thomas will take this as the basis of his explanation of the reasonableness of many beings. His non-being, however, will be neither that of Plato or Aristotle.

Plato, like Parmenides, made a conscious effort to study being as being. Unlike Parmenides, he refused to consider all that is as one immutable being. This fundamental rejection of monism helped Plato to perceive degrees of beauty and goodness in the beings of the universe. This more or lessness, or participation according to nature, indicated the existence of a being (idea) which as cause of all beauty and goodness was insusceptible of limitation. Plato was heir to Socrates' search for the universals, the essences of things which intellect apprehends and expresses in a definition. Acting upon this data, Plato inferred the extra-mental existence of a world of ideas which, being apprehended by the mind, constitute reality.

Plato accounted for the existence of material things by calling them participations or likenesses of the ideas. He would answer the problem of the individuation of being in terms of non-being. He agreed with Parmenides that absolute non-being is nonsense,[1] and in its place adopted a relative non-being. One being or idea is not another. Non-being is thus otherness and since intelligible, is itself an idea, one of the five supreme genera. The idea is absolute being. It contrasts with matter which, as constantly becoming, in a certain sense is not.[2]

In one of the most subtle passages of pure dialectic to be found in philosophy, Plato depicts the participations of the supreme genera of being, other, identity, motion and rest, and in so doing, establishes both a claim to fame in history and an impediment to the solution of the problem of being. The first three genera are found in all being; they participate in and are predicated one of

---

[1] *Sophist,* 258c.
[2] *Ibid.,* 257b-259b.

another. Being is itself and not another. Other (non-being), is itself. Sameness or identity is being and is distinct from other beings.[3] " Without being clearly conscious of it, Plato had in this way disengaged the idea of being . . . from the idea of essence, this latter being considered entirely under its negative aspect, as the reason of otherness and relative non-being." [4] This all inclusive aspect of the essence restricted his solution to the scope of an essentialism. The negative aspect of the essence was to supply a key to future philosophers who attempted to answer Parmenides by showing that there can be multiplicity, that is, otherness, and consequently, participation and relativity of being which in itself is absolute. These philosophers were Aristotle and St. Thomas. The one criticized Plato's thought, the other seems, while criticizing it, to have adopted it, or at least, corrected its error and made explicit what was only implicit in the *corpus platonicum.*

In St. Thomas' thought, there is a participation theory and many would say that it has come from Plato. Whether the inspiration was directly Platonic or the result of the Saint's own individual approach to reality, the theory itself is as meaningful as being itself. In St. Thomas' mind it is the most rational explanation of the being of experience. It is so meaningful precisely because it is so existential. Consequently, if Plato's limit proves to play a vital role in a Christian theory of participation, it will only do so after undergoing radical changes of meaning. Essentialism must be displaced by an existentialism. The significance of any theory of participation is determined by the signification of its notion of being. Plato's notion of being signifies the being of an essence, form or idea. The God of Christianity is no mere idea and He is being *par excellence.*

Plato's philosophy may rightly be termed an essentialism because its basic reality is that of essence, the Platonic ideas. They are real only as participations of the reality of the ideas. Platonic philosophy is a step towards the solution of the problem of the one and the many in the realm of being insofar as it is a conscious effort to cope with the problem in a truly philosophical manner. Unfortunately for Plato, and fortunately for the history of phi-

---

[3] *Ibid.,* 258e-259a.
[4] L. De Raeymaeker, *The Philosophy of Being,* p. 118.

losophy, the problem remains; for the nature of the relationship of the ideal and the real being is left unexplained by Plato. We are not told how the ideas may be separate from the participation and thus capable of existence as pure essences. More significantly, since no adequate explanation of the union of particular with ideal is given, we are left without an adequate explanation of the reality of the beings we experience, and thus are provided with science which cannot explain its own data. Plato brings us face to face with the problem of individuation, and yet loses the individual in the class. As in all idealisms, the many are lost in the one. The search for the being of the one among the many must take us through paths travelled in the history of philosophy by those who have their feet on the ground. We shall walk first with Aristotle.

Chapter III

ARISTOTLE'S MATERIAL AND FORMAL CAUSE

1. The Material Cause

Matter in General.

Both efficient and final causes are ultimately reduced to the formal cause. The same can be said of the material cause.[1] We are now in the presence of intrinsic causes, those which modify the being from within the very nature of the thing. The two intrinsic principles are deduced from the change of being. As stated above the matter is intelligible only in terms of the form. Matter, like efficiency, must be explained in terms of form. Both, however, are deduced from change, not from form. Matter and form, by this very fact, are not entirely within the scope of modern empirical science. Commencing his scientific investigation from the empirical fact of change, Aristotle is led by analogy to the notion of absolutely indeterminate matter to which form corresponds as its act.[2] From the fact of the change in the notions of the bronze and the figure, the physicist studies the matter and form of material moving bodies. Aristotle has arrived at the notions of matter and form. As such, these principles are not within the scope of modern empirical science. Such realities are not immediately observable. They are not even experimentally observable, as are such infinitesimal realities as the electron, proton, and photon of contemporary nuclear physics. But they (matter and form) are the particular object of Aristotelian natural philosophy which is concerned with material moving bodies. Aristotle observes, however, that physics concentrates more upon the form and studies the matter only insofar as it is required as a *quasi* means to the end that is the realization of the form.[3]

[1] *Metaph.*, H. 6, 1045a29-30.
[2] *Ph.*, I, 7, 191a7-12.
[3] *Metaph.*, E. 1, 1025b27.

Matter as Determinable Substrate and Privation.

Matter is evidence of change.[4] All things that change have matter, but different matter.[5] We have already spoken at length [6] of the fact of change as the basis for the reasoned existence of matter and form. There must always be a subject in every change. Whatever comes to be is a composite of substrate (matter) and form, that is, that which the substrate acquires; for example, a man becomes a musician. Aristotle views the subject of change as a contrary. Since contraries cannot act upon one another we can see the subject as it properly is that is, as the substratum which survives change.[7]

This substratum can be understood to mean matter or form, or the composite of both.[8] The Stagirite speaking in terms of the example of a statue, its shape, and the bronze of it, suggests that all three, that is, individual composite, its form, and its matter, are substrate. Of all three matter best qualifies as substrate, but least qualifies as οὐσία or substance.[9] In fact in *Book Z* of the *Metaphysics*, matter is contrasted with οὐσία.[10] Aristotle insists that it is impossible to equate οὐσία and substrate. Despite the inconsistencies [11] of terminology, the Stagirite seems to insist that matter is not οὐσία in the strict connotation of that word.[12] Matter is sub*strate*, not sub*stance*. It alone conforms to the strict definition of substrate.[13] The individual conforms only in a qualified manner. Form does not comply with the definition; in no way is it determinable. It is the source of an individual's determinacy. Ellen Stone Haring brings this out well, observing that although " form is not substrate in the standard sense of the term, it is οὐσία, a foundation of another kind." [14] As with the other causes, so with

---

[4] *Ibid.*, Z. 7, 1032a15-25.
[5] *Ibid.*, Λ. 2, 1069b25.
[6] Cf. pp. 67-71 in the original manuscript.
[7] *Ph.*, I, 6.
[8] *Metaph.*, H. 1, 1042a25-32.
[9] Ross, *Aristotle's Metaphysics*, pp. 159-160.
[10] *Metaph.*, Z. 3, 1029a19-24.
[11] Cf. *Ibid.*, 11, 1037b1-7.
[12] Ross, *Aristotle's Metaphysics*, II, p. 165.
[13] *Metaph.*, Z. 3, 1028b36-37.
[14] E. M. Stone, " Substantial Form in Aristotle's Metaphysics," *The Review of Metaphysics*, X (1956), p. 315.

matter; form is active and ultimate, matter is passive and undetermined.

The description of prime matter as something indeterminate is the result of a strict logical process. Aristotelian thought betrays a definite parallelism between thought and being. In consequence of this, the separate elements of the logical proposition become real components of the individually existing thing. In the logical proposition all the determination found in the predicate refers to the form. In the transition to the real order, then, matter is deprived of the character of being; it is a certain nonbeing, but it is not nothing.

Matter is to be distinguished from privation. Aristotle makes this clear.[15]

Matter and privation are indistinguishable in a given subject, yet conceptually different. Since matter is never without privation because union with one form denotes the deprivation of all other forms, matter and form are indistinguishable in reality. Since privation may be conceived as the absence of some thing in a subject, matter and form are conceptually different.

Privation also is related to form. It is actually the deprivation of a form in a substrate. It is, therefore, not a third element (a being) in becoming.[16]

In solving the difficulty, Aristotle distinguishes between essential and incidental connections, or what we would call things connected either *per se* or *per accidens*.[17] Considering this distinction in terms of the distinction between substrate and privation in *Physics VII*, we are able to see how what comes to be comes from both being and nonbeing. Whatever comes into being comes from nonbeing, but not precisely as nonbeing, in much the same way as the house comes from a doctor who builds it, but from him as house builder rather than doctor.

St. Thomas makes this notion a little clearer by distinguishing being *per se* and being *per accidens*. Matter is being *per se*; it is a principle of being. Privation on the other hand is being *per accidens*; it is equivalent to non-being.[18] To be yet more accurate, " matter has no actual existence but only a potential existence. It

[15] *Ph.*, I, 9, 192a3-5.   [17] *Ibid.*, I, 8, 191a35-b10.
[16] *Ibid.*, II, 1, 195b20.   [18] St. Thomas Aquinas, *S. T.*, I, 66, 2.

is thus the medium (*quasi* medium) between pure non-being and actual being." [19] Matter includes the notions of definability and capacity to receive opposites.[20] It has no autonomous existence. It exists only in a composite as the basis of the changes that take place in sensible things.

" Matter is the first substratum from which, as from a co-principle every being takes its origin; it is that which is indestructible, the permanent recipient of all opposites, the mother of all being." [21] Like artistic matter, it is passive and undetermined. " It can be spoken of neither as substance, quantity, nor any other kind of being." [22]

Definitions and Some Types of Matter

In keeping with the previous distinctions, matter may be defined either negatively or positively. Matter is " that which in itself is neither a particular thing nor a certain quantity nor assigned to any other of the categories by which being is determined." [23] Of itself matter is completely indeterminate. As such, it is the substrate which is receptive of generation and corruption. Thus, Aristotle defines it positively as " the primary substratum of each thing from which it comes to be without qualification, and which persists in the result." [24]

Aristotle distinguishes various types of matter. The notion of indeterminate matter described above should not be taken to exclude matter of some determination.[25] In this vein Aristotle speaks of primary and secondary matter.[26]

The expression ' prime matter,' used in the foregoing text, occurs at rather rare intervals in the *corpus aristotelicum*. The commentators, however, in acclaiming prime matter as the most important implication of Aristotle's thought, bear explicit testimony to its

[19] St. Thomas Aquinas, *In I Physicorum Aristotelis*, Lect. 9, 60.

[20] St. Thomas Aquinas, *In XII Metaphysicorum Aristotelis*, Lect. 2, 2428-2431.

[21] Aristotle, *De Gener. et Corr.*, I, 4; *Physics*, III, 4, 6.

[22] Aristotle, *Metaph.*, Z. 3.

[23] *Ibid.*, 1029a20.

[24] *Ph.*, I. 9, 192a31.

[25] Ross, *Aristotle's Metaphysics*, II, p. 234. Cf. *Metaph.*, H. 4, 1044a15.

[26] *Ibid.*, Θ. 7, 1049a26.

Aristotelian authenticity. Prime matter nowhere exists apart; it is only an element in the nature of individual concrete things composed of matter and form. " Only prime matter is entirely passive; other matter has some *quality* of its own and can thus initiate movement." [27]

Prime matter is the undetermined substrate. Second matter, on the other hand, is the individualized matter, the composite, the ' this ' of Aristotelian terminology. Secondary matter is matter already possessed of the positive determination of some form. [28] We have had occasion previously [29] to notice the ambiguity which exists in the Stagirite's notion of substance. Sometimes it is that which in things most truly is. At other times substance is equated with the individual which most truly is because it exists in itself and not in any other. The distinction between prime and secondary matter then becomes comparable to substrate as equivalent to composite of matter and form, or as absolutely undetermined matter.

2. The Formal Cause

Aristotle's Theory of Form as Being

Form is the cause of being. [30] Formal cause and act of substance coincide. [31] The form is that principle in virtue of which things are one in species while different in number, " the so-called ' formal nature,' which is specifically the same (though this is in another individual) ; for man begets man." [32] Form is identical with the thing, [33] although form in itself is neither singular nor universal. [34] Form is the act of sensible matter; as such, it is the cause of the being of the singular entity. Activating a mind, it is equivalent to the definition of the sensible thing. In this wise, it is potentially universal and capable of application to all of the species. [5]

[27] Ross, *Aristotle's Metaphysics*, II, p. 190; cf. *Metaph.*, Z. 9, 1034a11.
[28] *Metaph.*, Δ. 4, 1015a7-10.
[29] Cf. note 9.
[30] *Metaph.*, Z. 17, 1041b25-28; H. 2, 1043a2.
[31] J. Owens, *The Doctrine of Being in the Aristotelian Metaphysics*, p. 123.
[32] *Metaph.*, Z. 7, 1032a24-25.
[33] *Ibid.*, 1032b1-2; 14.
[34] *Ibid.*, 8, 1033b22; 10, 1035b14.
[35] *Ibid.*, 12, 1037b29-1038a30; M. 9. 10.

Aristotle identifies form and essence. He states that some things are causes " as the substratum (e. g. the parts) ; others as the essence (the whole, the synthesis, and the form)." [36] This text indicates also that form is a cause, the cause of being in the Aristotelian sense of that term. Existence is something given ; the problem is to determine why the matter is some particular thing.[37]

Aristotle definitely refers his four causes to the science of being *qua* being (which Fr. Owens calls ' Entity '),[38] but this reference is to a nature and not to an act of existence. The causes refer to the first category, i. e., substance. With entity, the four causes extend to all beings. Thus, although the causes do not pertain to any one genus, they have the necessary unity through their reference to entity.[39]

The Aristotelian causes can be said to refer to being, that is, actually to be causes of being or to contribute to the existence of things only insofar as they refer to form. But since the Aristotelian form pertains to essence rather than to existence, an analysis of Aristotle's four causes indicates that his approach to the theory of being is essentialistic rather than existentialistic. Causality is a contribution to essence, a form of existence only. Being means this or that kind of being. Hamlet's concern was not Aristotle's. ' To be or not to be ' is not the question. ' What to be? ' is the concern of every Aristotelian being. Aristotle does not distinguish the existential ' is ' from the copulative,[40] and thus he equates the existential and substantial orders and indicates that his metaphysics is essentialistic.

He has no question regarding existence or, more properly, the act of existence, although in an exceptional text of the *Posterior Analytics* he seems to recognize a difference between what a thing is and the fact that it exists.

Aristotle's notion of being is developed in terms of form. Being (form) is a perfection that can be predicated of all that exists

---

[36] *Ibid.*, Δ. 2, 1013b23.

[37] *Ibid.*, Z. 17, 1041b3-11.

[38] Owens, p. 169; cf. *Metaph.*, K. 3, 1061a8-9.

[39] Owens, p. 157.

[40] Ross, *Aristotle's Metaphysics*, I, p. 308; cf. *Metaph.*, Δ. 7, 1017a22.

simply because it exists. Aristole was keenly aware of this, even though his notion of being leaves something to be desired from the existential point of view. Since being applies to all that is, Aristotle's notion of being as form is incomprehensible unless this notion of being be understood in terms of a group of equivocals.[41] The Stagirite calls them πρός ἑν equivocals referring to one basic notion, that of form. This is Aristotle's " analogy " of being.

The Stagirite does not seem to have a well-developed doctrine of analogy. He calls things that are in some ways the same and in some ways diverse " equivocal " (πολλαχῶς λεγόμενα). The notion is a fundamental and recurrent one in Aristotelian thought. The Stagirite's metaphysical concepts thus indicate equivocal things having litle or no other function than to mirror their form. The notion of πρός ἑν equivocity is of especial importance to an understanding of Aristotle's notion of being, which, as we shall see later, is to be understood as a group of these πρός ἑν equivocals.

Descriptive purposes might indicate that a comparison with the scholastic analogy of attribution or proportion, is in order. Insofar as there is some element of equivocation in the scholastic attribution, we may say that what Aristotle regards as equivocals by reference (πρός ἑν), might be roughly equivalent to attribution which is usually conceived in terms of the reference of many things, improperly, to one Prime Analogate which possesses that perfection by its nature. Furthermore, what Aristotle considers as equivocals by analogy (as the analogy between substance and accidents), would then be equivalent to the scholastic analogy of proportionality. Such comparisons are not completely without merit, but should not, however, be considered as indicative of a well-developed theory of analogy of being in Aristotle's thought.[42] Therefore, in the light of this fundamental distinction, there can be no real equation of the Aristotelian with the scholastic notions of analogy.

Although objecting strenuously to the idea as the really real (ὄντως ὤν) of the Platonic world, Aristotle's own really real being is not so much the sensible object itself as the substantial form within the object.[43] From what we have seen of Aristotle's thought

[41] Owens, pp. 55-57.

[42] Cf. pp. 74-75; 96, n. 65 of the original manuscript, and J. Owens, pp. 58-60; 396, n. 14.

[43] *Metaph.*, Z. 1. 1028b2-8.

on this point is it but a simple procedure to equate the following notions: what primarily is, substance, that which is, what the thing is. And we can conclude that it is the whatness of a thing which constitutes its being and is identical with it. That which is most real in substance must be that by which it is in act. That by which it is in act, or its cause, is form. Form is an inner principle of being which accounts for the organic character of thing, their accidents, their operations and their very being. Once again Aristotelian philosophy brings to the fore its distinctive feature, the primacy of form. This insistent ubiquitousness of form may be reason enough to consider, as the specific form of Aristotelian philosophy itself, the fact that it seems to " know no act superior to form, not even existence." [44]

By way of summary and conclusion, it is well to note that a fairly coherent, if rather subtle, notion of being appears in the pages of the *Metaphysics*. The focal point is the τὸ τί ἦν εἶναι—the intelligible form which is at once the being and perfection of the thing. There is as subtle and as frequent a transfer from the logical to the metaphysical order in the *Metaphysics* of Aristotle as in the *De Ente et Essentia* of St. Thomas Aquinas. Both Aristotle and Aquinas agree that each of the two sciences must make its contribution to the notion of essence. In the natural order form is contrasted with matter and the matter-form composite. In the logical order the form is specific difference in contrast to the determination of the genus.

Not to be confused or identified with the τὸ τί ἦν εἶναι is the τὸ τί ἐστιν, the 'what it is.' The former is the necessary and immutable essence intelligible to the intellect; the latter is the thing considered as identified with its matter and form. Matter and form are included in the 'what it is.' [45] Matter, however, unintelligible in itself and the reason for change, is not included in a thing's quiddity or intelligible essence (τὸ τί ἦν εἶναι). [46]

All four causes should be reduced to formal cause. Aristotle has identified form with the primary instance of being, and so efficient,

---

[44] Gilson, *Being and Some Philosophers*, p. 47.
[45] Owens, p. 93; Robin, *Aristote*, p. 88.
[46] A. Maurer, " Form and Essence in the Philosophy of St. Thomas," *Mediaeval Studies*, 13 (1951), 172.

final, and material causes are in a sense reduced to formal causes. This is the extent of the relation between the Stagirite's theory of causes and his theory of being. Wisdom (Metaphysics) then will be the science of the formal cause. Form, therefore, is the highest degree of knowability. " Inasmuch as it was described as dealing with the first causes and that which is in the highest sense object of knowledge, the science of *substance* must be of the nature of Wisdom." [47] This "would indicate that the formal cause is the primary instance of knowability and that all the other causes are scientifically knowable only through it." [48]

The primary instance of *being* in the world is οὐσία, taken to mean substantial individuality. As such it provides the perspective for the whole causal theory. Every οὐσία we experience is in effect the localization of a form, a form which is constitutive of a being, the reason for essential functioning and the source of all its energies. In this wise it is capable of possessing diverse modes and being the organizational end of a multiplicity of products. The beings of our experience, men, stones, and the like, are plurality; yet, we must consider them, as a unit, as constituted by a sort of nucleus, a common nature of being, understood in terms of separate substance; and individually, as singular points of a causal reference which is primarily that of a formal cause. " The Aristotelian world is, from the beginning, a system of these centers of causal reference." [49] It must be noted, however, that these causal references are causes of change. There is no further reference to an act of existence.

Conclusion.

There is then, no application of potency and act in terms of essence and existence in Aristotelian philosophy because there is no realization of the distinct contribution of act of existence to real being. There is consequently, a basic lack of precision in Aristotle's solution of the problem of individuation and no attention at all given to the problem of individuality. There is a basic indi-

[47] *Metaph.*, B. 2, 996b14.
[48] Owens, p. 122.
[49] Dubarle, " La Causalité dans la philosophie d'Aristote," in *Recherches de Philosophie* I: Histoire de la Philosophie et Metaphysique, p. 48.

viduation in matter but since there is no attention paid to the act of existence, there is nothing to account for the separate and distinct existence of beings.

Aristotle attempted to remove the antinomy between experience of intrinsic change and its alleged impossibility which Parmenides and Democritus could not explain away. For Aristotle, as for Plato before him, being meant remaining the same, either as a form (Aristotle), or as an idea (Plato). Aristotle thought he could solve the problem of change by an analysis of being and by his theory that matter is intrinsically composed of a material and formal principle and that this composition makes change an essential characteristic of matter.

Aristotle was primarily interested in the causes of changing being. Each of his causes is a cause to the extent that it refers to the form of a thing. Causality represents a contribution to forms of existence and not to existence itself. St. Thomas Aquinas recognized that both Plato and Aristotle spoke of a cause of the substantiality of beings, but observes that they nowhere speak of the cause of the existence of these substances.[50]

The conception of causality is further evidence of Aristotle's purely physical approach to the matter-form theory. We cannot agree with Van Melsen [51] that Aristotle's notion of matter and form, despite what the Stagirite thought, was applied on the metaphysical level. It was, as we have seen, conceived in terms of change and always applied in terms of various aspects of changing being. A notion of causality limited to forms of existence and a theory of matter and form limited to change, is a definite indication of a finite metaphysics with its consequent lack of any theory of participation in being and a corresponding failure to offer any thorough-going explanation of the individuation and especially the individuality of beings.

[50] *Summa Theologiae*, I, 44, 2; cf. Gilson, *Spirit of Mediaeval Philosophy*, p. 440.
    [51] A. G. Van Melsen, *The Philosophy of Nature*, pp. 45-46.

CHAPTER IV

SAINT THOMAS' MATERIAL AND FORMAL CAUSE OF BEING

1. The Material Cause

Matter as Cause

The causality of matter is essentially correlative to that of form. Any description of one necessarily involves mention of the other. We will, however, make very brief mention of St. Thomas' notion of material cause, attempting to show (as we have done with the other causes) in what manner it influences being. For the rest the reader may be referred to the previous discussion of Aristotle's notion of matter. To a great extent our basic source with regard to material and formal causes will be St. Thomas' earliest work, the *De Ente et Essentia* for the central point at issue in this work is the metaphysical notion of matter and form. In opposition to the notion of universal matter developed by the Arabian Avicebron,[1] and adopted by St. Augustine, St. Thomas Aquinas attempts to show that these principles are proportionate to a metaphysical account of the hierarchy of created being. The question is especially pertinent to the problem of the nature of the separate substances (angels) and the human soul. Professor Gilson believes that the Angelic Doctor was directing his remarks especially against the Augustinians, Alexander of Hales and St. Bonaventure.[2]

St. Thomas' notion of matter as one of the causes of being is rooted in Aristotle's theory. Preliminary investigations reveal similarity in terminology and even in application, at least on the physical level. But similarities do not constitute identity of meaning.

---

[1] Cf. *De Ente et Essentia*, iv (*ad primum*); Avicebron, *Fons Vitae*, III, 18, p. 118.

[2] Gilson, *La Philosophie de S. Bonaventure*, pp. 234, 305; cf. also, J. Goheen, *The Problem of Matter and Form in the " De Ente et Essentia " of St. Thomas Aquinas*, p. 6, n. 10.

The truism is perhaps nowhere verified more forcefully in philosophy than in a comparison of the Angelic Doctor's notion of matter and form with the traditional Aristotelian hylomorphism. The differences are apparent from the first in a chronological reading of St. Thomas' writings. The failure on the part of so many Thomists through the centuries to recognize the fundamnetal difference would seem to indicate that the *De Ente et Essentia* is an insignificant little work rather than the first and foremost statement of Christian existentialism in the annals of the history of philosophy. From the very outset St. Thomas insists that the essence of material beings is neither matter nor form but a composite of both.[3] Later in the same work he makes it clear that this composite essence is itself to be considered as potential to act of existence.[4] We shall have more to say of this elsewhere.

Aristotle had spoken of being in terms of essence, or form, and form was act, in the sense of the act of matter. St. Thomas, as we have seen, identifies being with act of existence. The *esse* is the act of the essence which is to be considered as potential to existence. This same essence is a composite of matter (potential essence), and form, which makes it an actual essence. Matter is no longer eternal, but created. The emphasis is necessarily placed upon the bestowal of existence, upon *beings* rather than natures. In this context, matter and form, traditionally considered since the time of the Stagirite as the principles of nature, take on an added significance, an existential connotation.

We must urge caution at the beginning lest this treatment which separates matter and form for purposes of study, result on the one hand, in the substantialization of either or both, or on the other, recognition of them as existing half-beings of a whole. St. Thomas insists that as the material and formal causes of being, matter and form are principles of being and not themselves beings.[5] It is obvious, therefore, that treatment of one obviously involves mention of the other. St. Thomas takes cognizance of these two aspects when describing prime matter. Since definition is through the form, prime matter cannot be defined itself (*per se*), but only

[3] *De Ente,* II, 4.
[4] *Ibid.,* IV, V.
[5] *In II Sent.,* D. 3, 1, 6c.

through the composite. Thus, we can say that prime matter holds itself as unfigured (unformed) brass to idol with regard to all forms and privations.[6] Prime matter, then, is to be defined in terms of pure potency. Considered devoid of all its distinguishing forms and privations, prime matter is one in all bodies. It is pure potency and as such, does not exist because form is act and it (matter) is devoid of act.[7] This is the matter that will interest us here; for, it is a principle of being.[8] It may, in a manner of speaking, be considered as infinite, that is, without limit, and made finite by form.[9] It is called " prime " to differentiate it from second or sensible matter, that is, the matter of objects possessed of form, which may be considered either as common or individual, depending upon whether informed by the form of the species (the universal), or by the particular forms, thus designating respectively, the class essence and the particular essence.[10] Matter exists only as it is designated in corporeal substances. It acquires *esse* actually insofar as it acquires form. It is through the form that the substance becomes the proper subject of that which is the *esse.*[11] Matter, however, is created by God concreated with form. The real subject of creation is neither taken singly, but the determinate being as composite of matter and form.[12] Since species do not exist except in the individuals of the class, individuals are individuated by the material element of their essences, namely, by sensible designated matter with its proper quantity in which the accidents inhere.[13] Matter, then, distinguishes the individual while form determines the diversity of the species. Matter is the principles of numerical difference; form the principle of specific difference. The effect of the causality of matter is individual being, whereas the formal cause determines the being in its species.[14] The reciprocity of material

[6] *De Principiis Naturae,* ch. 2, 345.
[7] *De Spiritualibus Creaturis,* 1c.
[8] Cf. above note 5.
[9] *St. T.,* I, 7, 3c.
[10] *Ibid.,* I, 85, 1, ad 2.
[11] *Ibid.,* 75, 6.
[12] *De Pot.,* 3, 1, ad 12.
[13] *De Ente,* II, 7.
[14] *C. G.,* II, 53.

and formal causes in the process of individuation is an application of the reciprocity of potency and act. Matter is passive potency, the possibility for multiplication of the form. More complete presentation of individuation and its consequences is reserved for the following chapter. The manner of the causality of matter will be the next concern.

St. Thomas' criterion for evaluation of the efficacy of any cause is, as we have seen, its contribution to, or influence upon, the being of a thing. Determination of the efficacy of the material cause necessarily involves its relationship to a formal cause; for, matter is causal with respect to form only, and in terms of the potency-act relationship.[15] Matter is a cause of existence to the extent that it offers itself up as the subject, recipient of the existence of a form. The form influences existence by elevating matter to the realm of actual being.[16] Matter, therefore, is the cause of form by existing as its subject, while form is the cause of the matter by conferring actuality upon it, their union being the result of the action of some efficient cause acting for an end.[17] Causing reciprocally and mutually in combination, matter and form constitute the essence. The essence in turn, receives its act of existence through the form as act of substance and together with the *existential* act of existence is the existing reality.

Because it is potential, matter is set off from all the causes.[18] It is this very potency that restricts matter from the realm of being and yet keeps it from the realm of pure non-being.[19] Matter is not an actual being, nor pure non-being; it is being *per accidens*. As non-actualized being, matter is incomplete (*incompletissimum inter omnia entia*),[20] for it does not enjoy autonomous existence. It exists only in composition with form and existence as the substratum of change and the subject of existence. Since matter enjoys only potential and no actual existence it is a sort of medium between pure non-being and actual being. St. Thomas calls such

---

[15] See chapter three of the original manuscript.
[16] More will be said of the causality of form in the following section.
[17] *S. T.*, I, 3, 7c.
[18] *In II Phys.*, Lect. XI, 242.
[19] *In I Phys.*, Lect. XIV, 127.
[20] *De Spirit. Creat.*, 1c.

potential beings *quasi-mediums*.[21] Identification of matter with
non-being, however, is an error attributed by St. Thomas to Plato
and Avicenna.[22]

We have spoken of the Platonic theory of matter at some
length;[23] it remains here only to present St. Thomas' views on
privation and its relation to the material cause, and the form.

Matter and Privation

"Privation" usually denotes the absence of something that is
due to a thing. Understood philosophically, the term denotes a
principle of nature. St. Thomas agrees with Aristotle [24] that the
principles of nature are three in number. We have observed that
cause and principle are not equated by St. Thomas. He logically,
then, considers only two intrinsic causes (matter and form), while
allowing that these are not the only principles of being.

The question here obviously is the problem of physical change.
The context is that of the traditional philosophical approach to
the problem in terms of the opposition of contraries.

Opposition may be considered either in terms of contradictories
or contraries.[25] Contradictions exist between two terms only; there
is no medium.[26] Contrary opposition, however, is between two terms
that are not mutually exclusive, even though they be in the same
genus,[27] and, therefore, includes a medium between the two terms.
Change, then, must involve contraries and at least three principles
because it is impossible for anything to come from just two contraries that are opposed to each other. In the process, each contrary
changes some third thing which is the subject of both. There
must be, then, some third being or principle of being, which exists
as the subject of the contraries in order that effects come to be
from the contraries. This third principle of becoming is privation
which contributes to becoming by placing some obstacle in the
subject which removes the power of the subject to act.[28]

[21] *In I Phys.*, Lect. IX, 60.
[22] *In VII Meta.*, Lect. 2.
[23] See Part I, Chapter Three of the original manuscript.
[24] See pages 69-72 of the original manuscript.
[25] *In V Meta.*, Lect. 12.   [27] *Ibid.*, Lect. 9, *passim*.
[26] *In X Meta.*, Lect. 6, 2042.   [28] *S. T.*, I, 11, 2.

It is privation that renders matter potential; for, it denotes a lack of a form that matter could have. Privation is only an accidental principle of nature but nevertheless, a real and necessary one.[29] It is accidental because it is identical in subject matter, negative in character, and, a principle of becoming as opposed to being. One in subject matter and associated with form in opposition to contrariety, it is the bond between matter and form in the process of becoming which results in a new form. With respect to form, privation is considered with form as one of the two contraries. Furthermore, the subject of these two contraries which is changed by them may be considered to be the form of the new being.[30] This, because privation always implies the absence of the form the subject is due to have, considered in opposition to the form it now has. With respect to matter, privation is the *raison d'être* of its potency; and yet, it is through privation that matter is moved from the realm of absolute to the realm of so-called accidental non-being. The influence of privation then is clearly seen to be only that of a principle of the becoming of a new being. Matter is potential to reality, as a principle of being it is " almost being "; whereas, privation is non-being.[31] Privation enters into the becoming but not the constitution of being, and hence, is properly called a principle of becoming but not an intrinsic cause of being.

In the light of these considerations, the sole reason for the existence of matter is that certain forms might determine it to themselves. " *Materia est propter formam.* "[32] Matter influences *esse* by being the support of form which is the vehicle of the act of *esse*. It remains now to determine St. Thomas' notion of formal causality and its particular contribution to existence. The relationship of matter and form is the topic that logically follows here. We have reserved treatment of this problem of mutual and reciprocal causality to the discussion of the principle of individuation.[33]

[29] *De Prin. Nat.*, II, 343.
[30] *In I Phys.*, Lect. X, *passim*.
[31] *S. T.*, I, 66, 2.
[32] *In I Phys.*, Lect. 1, 5.
[33] See Part III, Chapter Three, Section 3 of the original manuscript.

Matter and Metaphysics.

There is one further consideration with respect to material cause that is of consequence in the field of metaphysics. It is a theme that Professor Gilson has frequently developed.[34] We have seen that the notion of material causality taught by St. Thomas seems to have been adopted from Aristotle and closely resembles its traditional Aristotelian formulation. We have also observed in a previous chapter,[35] the similarities and differences between the Stagirite and the Angelic Doctor with respect to subject and method of the science of metaphysics. In each instance there was an extension and deepening of meaning given to the science by the Thomistic interpretation in the light of the content of Divine Revelation. The material cause is one of four proposed by Aristotle and St. Thomas alike as means of knowing being *qua* being. Here the similarity ceases. For Aristotle, matter was eternal and consequently lay outside the scope of the causes of being. Consequently, the ultimate knowledge of being through the causes cannot possibly attain to a first cause which is the cause of being; for, matter is anterior to such causal considerations of the first cause and remains unexplained by the god of Aristotle. " For this reason the metaphysics of Aristotle cannot be reduced to complete unity." [36]

The God of Aquinas, however, is the God of Christianity, He Who Is, the first and final cause of all that is. Metaphysics, therefore, as a science of being *qua* being through its ultimate causes, resolves itself to the rational science of the first Cause, Being Itself (*Ipsum Esse Subsistens*). Metaphysics now orientated to the knowledge of God as the final, as well as the efficient cause of all that is, truly becomes a divine science.[37]

We have seen earlier in this work, how this divine science of Aristotle focused upon the notion of form in its various different expressions—the πρός ἐν equivocals—ultimately focusing upon the separate forms or entities, as the most noble instances of form. We must now conclude this chapter with an investigation of St.

[34] Gilson, *Being and Some Philosophers*, pp. 154-157.
[35] See Part III, Chapter One, Section 6 of the original manuscript.
[36] Gilson, *Being and Some Philosophers*, p. 156.
[37] *C. G.*, III, 25.

Thomas' notion of form. It is here that the greatest differences between the Aristotelian and Thomistic metaphysics lie.

2. *The Formal Cause*

The Notion of Form.

Form in General. The last, and perhaps the most important aspect of causality as far as this thesis is concerned, is the contribution to existence made by the form. As with Aristotle, so with Aquinas, the notion of form is one of wide application and meaning. Form may be equivalent to figure,[38] a type of argumentation,[39] a verbal sacramental formula,[40] the essential principle of knowability and definition,[41] or formal causality (our one and only concern here). In a memorable passage of his *Commentary on the Metaphysics*, St. Thomas focuses our attention on that aspect of form which will be our concern in the next few pages.[42]

The form, then, is that which is in things as the principle of their determinations,[43] whether they be accidental or essential. As we shall see, the term form is highly analogous. It is used by St. Thomas in reference to material composite substances and separated intelligences or forms as well. Both applications are made in view of the fundamental causal significance of forms.

The standard lexicons to St. Thomas' writings list several pages of references indicating various aspects of formal causality.[44] In keeping with the theme of this chapter, we have selected from this variety of meanings a few aspects of formal causality which we believe to be most indicative of the peculiar influence upon existence contributed by form as a cause.

On the level of the human experience a few aspects of formal causality give us an insight into this fundamental meaning. Besides the aspect of exemplarism, already discussed, St. Thomas speaks

---

[38] *In IV Sent.*, D. 1, 1, 3, ad 2.
[39] *In I Anal.*, 8, 72 *bis.*
[40] *C. G.*, IV, 74.
[41] *In I Periherm.*, 8, 96.
[42] *In V Meta.*, Lect. 2.
[43] *In III Sent.*, D. 27, 1, 1c.
[44] L. Schütz, *Thomas-Lexikon*, pp. 315-322.

in terms of formal causality of forms as accidental, substantial, material and intelligible. In the realm of the conceivable, he speaks of the pure forms that are the separated intellectual substances.[45] Since his description of the angels provides us with St. Thomas' most distinct and unique notion of form, we shall reserve a few later pages for treatment of this specific point. Meanwhile, for descriptive purposes, we should say a few words regarding the nature of accidental and substantial material forms. Broadly speaking, their function is to give being to matter in the manner described earlier in our treatment of the material cause.

The Individuation of Form.

The Individuation of Form. It has been indicated that form gives beings their species. The form, then, must be the same in each of a kind. How, then, do the many of a given class exist and remain aloof as distinct individuals? Complete discussion of the problem of individuation must be reserved for the final chapter on the " Limitation of Existence." Presently, completion of the portrayal of St. Thomas' notion of form demands mention that reference be made to matter as the principle which makes the universal form an individual. The common element of individuals of a class is *specifically* the same; for they all possess the same form. Also, however, they are *numerically* distinct. Enumeration could not be from the form which is one.[46] Numerical enumeration must have its basis in quantity, an accident of matter.[47] Thus St. Thomas holds that *materia quantitate signata* is the cause of individuation. Note that it is not quantity itself which is an accident, and consequently cannot be the cause of the subject in which it inheres—but quantified matter, that it, matter with dimensions, which individuates. Thus, dimensified, matter is called " *signata.*" [48]

This matter is not the determining principle, however, for no matter can be accidentally modified unless it exists actually as informed.[49] As form is multiplied in matter, so does matter while

---

[45] *S. T.*, III, 13, 1c.
[46] *Ibid.*, I, 3, 2, ad 3.
[47] *De Ver.*, 2, 6, ad 1.
[48] *In Boet. de Trin.*, IV, 2c.
[49] *In I Sent.*, D. 8, 5, 2c; *In II Sent.*, D. 30, 2, 1c.

multiplying, individuate forms. The question of the virtual or potential pre-existence of perfections and dispositions in matter has already been discussed.[50] They are to be understood, says St. Thomas, as accidents on the way to generation—*in via generationis*.[51] The result of this generation is a new individual. The emphasis upon matter as principle of individuation should not detract from the primacy of form. Individuals owe more to their form than to their matter. Form is the principle of determination of those very material notes which individuate beings. Matter individuates the form by receiving it into itself, thereby designating the individual. The problem of individuality and individuation will be discussed in our final chapter. There the existential import of this doctrine will be evident.

The Causality of Form

St. Thomas, Form, Essence and Substance. The identification of these terms in Aristotelian thought, as well as the importance given these notions in previous chapters, demand an introductory note on their use by St. Thomas Aquinas.

Our treatment of individual causes has shown the interrelation of the various causes both extrinsic and intrinsic, and other phases of the treatment of matter and form have described facets of the mutual and reciprocal causality of these two intrinsic causes. The present discussion of the causality of form involves the relation of, or better, the contribution made by, form to essence and to existence. Like all phases of the causality of form, the problem at hand centers round the notion of form as act. The all pervasiveness of this notion of form which has gradually become ever more obvious, now culminates in these two final sections. Here the differences between Aristotle and St. Thomas will become most apparent; for, form will no longer be identified with essence, and will make a very definite, although qualified, contribution to existence.

For Aristotle, form was the primary instance of being; all the causes contributed something to the being of the form. Form itself gave the nature and entity of the being and was itself identical with the essence. Aristotle's direct application of act and potency

[50] See pages 269-270 of the original manuscript.
[51] *C. G.*, II, 71.

to form and matter confirmed this position. Essence for the Stagirite was form which determined prime matter to a definite substance by a process of information. It is then, more proper to speak of Aristotle's being in terms of substance, for this is the effect of form's causality upon matter. Thus Aristotle has written that " the form, or the thing as having form (i. e. substance) should be said to be the thing." [52] Aristotelian form, considered as act, does not contribute to, rather it is identified with, the really existent thing. St. Thomas' notion, although couched in much the same phraseology, presents a considerably different aspect of form as act.

Form, in composite substances, is a part of the essence or quiddity, that is, the essence viewed as definition. For essence is what the definition of a thing signifies and the definition of physical substances includes both matter and form thus differentiating them from mathematical definitions.[53] Neither matter, because it is unknowable pure potency, nor form alone, can be the essence; for, a thing is knowable through its essence.[54] St. Thomas seems to have adopted this doctrine from Avicenna. Having stated it in the *De Ente*, he insisted upon it throughout his career.[55] In commenting upon the *Metaphysics*, the Angelic Doctor attributes the doctrine to Aristotle.[56] Fr. Maurer, however, by superimposing text and commentary, has shown that by form (εἶδος), Aristotle means quiddity (τὸ τί ἦν εἶναι), as distinct from matter.[57] Fr. Maurer suggests that William of Moerbeke may have been responsible for St. Thomas' interpretation of Aristotle in terms of his (Thomas') own theory of matter and form. William translated Aristotle's εἶδος meaning quiddity τὸ τί ἦν εἶναι) with the Latin *species* which, with the matter, is said to constitute the whole.[58] Species includes at least the notion of universal matter and is distinct from form

---

[52] Aristotle, *Metaph.*, a, 9, 1035a6.

[53] *De Ente*, II, (*ad principium*).

[54] *Ibid.*, 5.

[55] *Compendium Theologiae*, 154; *C. G.*, IV, 81, and Maurer, " Form and Essence in the Philosophy of St. Thomas," *Mediaeval Studies*, XIII (1951), p. 169.

[56] *In VII Meta.*, Lect. 9, 1469; cf. Aristotle, *Metaph.*, Z. 10, 1035b32.

[57] Maurer, *Mediaeval Studies*, XIII (1951), p. 170.

[58] Spiazzi edition of St. Thomas' *Commentary on Metaphysics*, p. 361, 626.

alone. To say that the whole is composed of matter and form (*ex specie et materia*) signifies, according to St. Thomas, species existing in determined matter.[59] St. Thomas distinguishes between the meanings of *species* and *forma*; Aristotle does not. For Aristotle, "*species* is form (εἶδος), because it must be added to matter to form the composite whole; *it does not itself include matter*. Clearly St. Thomas must force Aristotle's text to have it say that matter is included in the *species*.[60]

St. Thomas, however, considering matter and form as principles of the essence which itself is in potency to existence (a point which we shall soon develop),[61] holds that the quiddity (*species*) of a material object includes universal matter. Consequently, when Aristotle speaks of an indeterminate matter that is separate from form (Aristotle's prime matter), St. Thomas understands him to speak of the individual matter which is not ordinarily included in the definition of things.[62] St. Thomas like Aristotle understands quiddity in terms of the definition of the essence [63] and frequently speaks of essence in the same way, thereby identifying essence and quiddity. Quiddity is that which the definition signifies. This quiddity, however, despite the Angelic Doctor's attributions to Aristotle,[64] is not the same as the Stagirite's. The Aristotelian quiddity (τὸ τί ἦν εἶναι), the definition of the essence—*quod quid erat esse* in Latin, is form alone, to which in the definition of material substance, matter is added. Further, St. Thomas states that essence and substance in composite substances designate a composite of matter and form.[65] Aristotle's substance (οὐσία) however, refers to matter, form, and composite, and obviously, is not the same as St. Thomas' notion of essence. St. Thomas' essence has a further relation to the act of existence: it is that principle in and by which a being holds its existence; not in form, nor matter alone but in composite.[66] For Aristotle, it is the form which as the primary

---

[59] *In VII Meta.*, Lect. 10, 1491.

[60] Maurer, *Mediaeval Studies*, XIII (1951), p. 171 (Italics added).

[61] This notion is elaborated in the following pages.

[62] *In VII Meta.*, Lect. 11, 1530.

[63] *De Ente*, II.

[64] *Ibid.*, I.

[65] *Ibid.*

[66] *Ibid.*, cf. *C. G.*, II, 43.

being inheres in matter as in its subject of existence. Form is act for both Saint and Stagirite but, as we shall now see, its activity varies considerably in their respective explanations of being.

Form as Act of Essence. Form is act; it makes a thing to be in act.[67] It is the actual term of production and the principle of a being's operation. It is that to which existence comes.[68] Insofar as a being enjoys being according to its form, it can be called a cause of *esse*.[69] Existence follows upon form, but not as the effect of an efficient cause;[70] for, it is a cause of substantial not existential being.[71] Form, then, is act and even primary act, but in the order of substance. Form makes a substance to be *what* it is; gives its specific nature making it this sort. Being, however, is due to the proper act of existence. Form, then, is an act but because not all acts are forms, its effect, substantial being (essence), remains potential to existence. " In short, forms are ' formal ' causes of existence, to the whole extent to which they contribute to the establishment of substances which are capable of existing." [72]

We have seen that the formal cause causes by a direct actualization of the potential principle, matter. Through this determination of matter, the form gives the specific being to matter—*forma dat speciem*. It is in the light of this scholastic axiom that the contribution of form to existence is to be understood. Form gives being to matter as its formal cause.[79] This feature of formal causality is frequently stated as *forma dat esse simpliciter*. Here is a real statement of position : it is not matter but form that determines the species. The axioms, however, could be easily misleading.

When we speak of form causing being we must ever bear in mind two facts already established. This causality is formal, not efficient; it is in the order of substance or essence, not the existential order. Since determination, that is, the limitation of matter in essence, denotes some perfection, form must be act of essence. Furthermore, and this is of utmost importance, form gives being

[67] *S. T.*, I, 75, 7c.
[68] *Ibid.*, 50, 5c.
[69] *Ibid.*, 75, 6c.
[70] *Q. D. De Anima*, 14, ad 4.
[71] *C. G.*, II, 54.
[72] Gilson, *Being and Some Philosophers*, p. 169; cf. *C. G.*, II, 54.
[73] *In I Sent.*, D. 8, 5, 2.

according to the order of which it is act. Therefore, in the order of substantial existing being, the form will determine *what* the act of existence will *be*. Form is a principle of existence, but only in relation to substance.[74] " The proper role of form is to constitute substance as *substance*. . . . Thus conceived form is *that by which* the substance is *that which is*. . . . This form is only the principle of existence to the extent that it achieves substance, which is that which exists." [75] There are, then, two orders: the order of substance or essence and the order of existence. There is an act corresponding to each order: formal act of essence determining what the thing is and entitative act of existence establishing the being as actual in distinction to the mere possibility for existence that is essence.

St. Thomas Aquinas agrees with Aristotle that the form is an actual cause of the existence of a composite. He does not, however, identify form and essence as Aristotle did. In fact, Thomas distinguishes form and matter. He holds that the essence is a composite of both.[76] Form as a principle of essence is one of the principles by which being exists. Form alone, however, is a cause of *esse* only as a formal cause giving existence to matter. Form is an act, the act of matter whose union with form produces a composite. This is as true for St. Thomas [77] as it was for Aristotle. But Aquinas held that the essence never really exists apart from existence. Whereas the Stagirite's being was substance or form, the Angelic Doctor's essence remains potential to yet another act. *Esse* replaces form as the most perfect of acts. Form makes the essence an actual essence but only the act of existence makes that essence exist.

Form is the quidditative act, that is, it determines matter to quiddity or to its distinctive species of being. The act of existence, however, is not the act of matter [78] but rather the *actus essendi* which determines essence to exist. The nature constituted of matter and form is potential to existence because it is receptive of existence. There is a twofold composition corresponding to the two acts

[74] *C. G.*, II, 54.
[75] Gilson, *The Christian Philosophy of St. Thomas Aquinas*, pp. 32-33.
[76] *De Ente*, II.
[77] *In II Metaph.*, Lect. 4, 320.
[78] *C. G.*, II, 54.

of composite created substance, the act of matter and the act of existence—two acts in one being. The one is sublimated to the other despite the fact that the one cannot exist without the other. They exist simultaneously. Form cannot determine matter without existence being received into the essence thereby perfecting it. The two remain distinct: act of existence is not act of form. The composition of form and act of existence in intellectual created substances ever remains the positive indication of the distinction of act of existence and act of form.[79] With the intelligible aspects of form sublimated to existence, matter is viewed less as a potentiality and more as in relation to existence as a principle of the composite of matter and form that is the recipient of existence. Matter becomes a necessity to the complete intelligibility of material substance. Here again, matter and form take up a more exalted place among the principles of being when matter is viewed not as eternal but as created. In fairness to the Stagirite, it must be observed that an inchoate tendency to integrate matter into the quiddity is found in his works. For, since " what is manifested by the definition of a material substance is a composite of matter and form, both must be embraced in that essence." [80] Armed with this insight of Aristotle, and motivated by the existential implications of the doctrine of creation, St. Thomas integrated form and matter in the essence. Essence, however, for St. Thomas, never really exists apart from existence except in mental processes.[81] Essence, then, is not being, it is potential to being. In this light, it is possible that form has a further contribution to existence; this time a potential one.

In a Christian metaphysics of being, essence is activated by, and is itself, primarily form. Existence, not essence, is reality; and, existence makes form to be. In a material being existence makes form to be and matter exists in virtue of this existing form. Form gives being to matter; for, form is the cause, act, and nature of the thing in which matter exists. Both matter and form contribute to existence in the sense that existence is, as it were, constituted by these principles of the essence.[82] A being has being by its form,[83]

[79] *De Spirit. Creat.*, 1 (*ad finem*).

[80] Maurer, *Mediaeval Studies*, XIII (1951), pp. 175-176; cf. Ross, *Aristotle's Metaphysics*, I, pp. civ, cvi, and Aristotle, *Metaph.*, Z. 10, 1035b25-26.

[81] *De Ente*, I.

[82] *In IV Meta.*, Lect. 2, 558.   [83] *S. T.*, I, 76, 7c; *C. G.*, II, 54.

but this is essential or substantial being to which existence itself comes. It is all a matter of understanding the causality of form as properly distinct from efficient causality. Form causes the thing to be what it is; an agent causes it to be. Form causes the *whatness*; efficient agents cause the *isness*. Again, there is a fundamental divergence between Aristotle and St. Thomas. All the Aristotelian causes focused upon form as the act of being; all other causality was sublimated to formal causality and consequently, whatness became beingness. In St. Thomas' writings all causality looks to efficiency and the bestowal of being; for, it is being itself (*ipsum esse*), and ultimately the Essential Existence Itself of God (*Ipsum Esse Subsistens*), that makes beings to be in act. Formal causality remains very real in Thomistic philosophy; the ubiquity of the term itself testifies to the fact. Nevertheless, formal causality has become very existential in virtue of its sublimation to efficient causality. This sublimation becomes a discernible fact when attention is focused upon the notion of form as act.

Cursory survey might easily lead to the assumption that St. Thomas treats of activity in the same manner as Aristotle. Form and act are expressions common to both. A being is active because it is in act. For Aristotle, this means that a being actively exists in act because its form, that is, its primary being, is actual. For St. Thomas, thinking in terms of *esse* as the perfection of all acts,[84] this statement indicates that beings actually exist, not solely because of their form, but especially because of their act of existence. St. Thomas agrees with Aristotle that existing beings act through their form as a principle of operation but insists that the form of an object is definitely not the existential act of that being.[85] This statement states the core of existential doctrine and the fundamental point of this thesis.

Form is being only in the sense of a principle of being.[86] Existence contributes to the being of all things, even forms. *Esse* is formal [87] of all in an existing thing but is not itself a form or essence. St. Thomas means to state that as form stands to matter,

---

[84] *De Pot.*, 7, 2, ad 9.
[85] *C. G.*, II, 54.
[86] *De Pot.*, 3, 8.
[87] *S. T.*, I, 4, 1, ad 3.

so existence stands to form.[88] Form is a cause of activity. Every agent causes through its form.[89] Through the form, things are brought into act.[90] Form is the principle of activity directive of the action, but always presupposes the act of existence, for existence is prior in nature to action—a thing must be before it can act. In the final analysis, therefore, form is indeed true act, but it is so called principally because of its intimate affiliation with *esse*, the act of existence. This affiliation is indicative of a certain potential character of form in the contribution to existence.

Form and Existence.

Both form and existence are considered by St. Thomas as perfection. Both are described as causes of existence. *Esse* is the greatest perfection, the actuality and cause of existence in all things.[91] It is the *actus essendi*, the act of being that is formal of everything that exists.[92] Furthermore, and this creates the problem, St. Thomas says that the form is a cause of being—*forma dat esse simpliciter*.[93] Both form and existence are called act and the cause of existence. How then, does the form fit in with existence? The answer to the question emphasizes the difference between Thomistic existentialism and Aristotelian essentialism by placing the form of being in its true perspective, that is, in its potential relation to the act of existence.

St. Thomas' solution rests upon the distinction of essence and existence and its extension to matter and form in the order of essence. Form and existence are not identical but they are nevertheless separable logically. In the real order, however, form and existence are inseparably associated because existence comes to and through the form. A thing possesses being only so long as it possesses its form.[94] Form is the medium for participation in existence.[95] But the fact that form is potential to existence does

[88] Gilson, *Being and Some Philosophers*, p. 170.
[89] *In III Phys.*, Lect. iv, 302.
[90] *C. G.*, I, 23, *passim*.
[91] *S. T.*, I, 4, 1, ad 3.
[92] *Ibid.*, 8, 1c.
[93] *Ibid.*, 76, 4c.
[94] *C. G.*, II, 55.
[95] *S. T.*, I, 65, 4c.

not mean that it is the subject of the *esse*. It remains only the principle by which a thing is.[96] Form is a principle of existence only to the extent that it is the act of the quiddity which is necessary for determined existence.[97] Existence therefore is the act and complement of form as it is of everything that exists, but is most intimately united to form as that by which it (existence) comes to a being. If existential philosophy should occasionally call form " act " it is only because existence follows immediately upon the form,[98] and because form is equivalent to an actual essence.

The uniquely Thomistic notion of form appears in all its clarity in St. Thomas' description of the nature of the intellectual substances.[99] Form has become receptive in character.[100] The potentiality of form signified by the granting of existing to separated substances is a further indication of the potentiality of form in the lower realms of material substance.[101]

The distinction of essence and existence has severely modified Aristotle's notion of form as being and act. St. Thomas sublimated the pure act which Aristotle called form to the act of existence which is attached to form in the very act of creation. Aristotle's pure forms are no longer eternal; their existence is given them by God. The only place where the Aristotelian form maintains any of its original character is in composite material substances where it gives existence to matter. But even here because the whole composite is in potency to the act of existence form loses much of its autonomous character.

Although St. Thomas makes the efficacy of the form depend upon the act of existence, form does not become less noble by that very dependency. As potential to existence it becomes the principle of the hierarchical structure of the universe, for beings are ranked according to the capacity of the receiving nature.[102] Difference in form, and consequently in essence, will determine the degree of the participation in existence.

[96] *Ibid.*
[97] *Ibid.*, 76, 7c.
[98] *De Spirit. Creat.*, I, 1c.
[99] *De Ente*, iv, 27.
[100] *Ibid.*, 28.
[101] *Ibid.*, v, 33.
[102] *Ibid.*, 31.

A recurring theme of this thesis and the basic indication of the unique position of the existentialism of St. Thomas Aquinas is the potentiality of form. This potentiality of form is as characteristic of Thomism as the actuality of form is of Aristotelianism. Herein lies the difference between the systems and the key to the complete solution of the problem of being. The unique contribution of St. Thomas to the solution of the problem of the one and many in the order of existence was to make form, of the order of essence, potential to the act of existence. Considered in the order of existence beings are composed of essence which limits existence. On the order of essence there is composition of matter limiting form. St. Thomas' solution was the result of his total view of being and an appreciation of the various contributions to existence made by the different causes. He realized that it is as necessary to explain being in terms of both essence and existence as it is to explain light in terms of both sun and medium. It is through the form that the act-of-being causes existence.[103] Form is the formal cause of existence as the formal cause of the substance to which existence comes. The form then is potential because it is the recipient of existence, but it is an active cause because it is a form.

A basic position of this dissertation is once again located in that area of discussion where the activity of causes contributing to existence indicate an existential note to the being which they cause. "The *esse* is that which is more intimate and more profound in anything, since it is the formal element of everything in the thing." [104] Act of existence enjoys a unique primacy because it gives being to all that exists,[105] even to formal causes.

Conclusion

By way of conclusion to this section on form we might indicate the salient features stressed in our presentation. Form is limited by matter, is individualized by it, existing in a multiplicity of individuals but retaining its uniformity in the process of generation and corruption. It is the principle of knowability. It confers existence, that is, a *certain form* of existence, and is the principle of

---

[103] *C. G.*, II, 54.
[104] *S. T.*, I, 8, 1c.
[105] *Ibid.*, 4, 1, ad 3.

activity in things which are able to act insofar as they are in act. All these things St. Thomas said, as did Aristotle before him. But in the *De Ente et Essentia*, St. Thomas introduced a new conception of form—a form with a mixture of potency. In order to show in just what manner form is potential, St. Thomas explained his distinction of essence and existence as the last step in his answer to Avicebron. This explanation of the limitation of being provides the topic of our final chapter.

CONCLUSIONS OF THE DISSERTATION

1. Regarding Matter and Form

The matter-form theory has come to be called " hylomorphism " from the Greek words for matter and form. As a theory explanatory of change and as a phase of the constitution of the hierarchical structure of being it is susceptible of application in both physics and metaphysics. It may be a thoroughly physical theory explaining change or it may be an aspect of the metaphysical explanation of the individuality of being. Aquinas used the theory in both physical and metaphysical science, always, however, emphasizing its primary metaphysical character.

Physics treats of corporeal elements in motion and the various forms of the genesis of being. St. Thomas used hylomorphism to solve these problems of what was called the physics of his day. In the solution of the problem of change matter is potential essence. It is determinable and signifies more of the essence yet to come in the process. Matter is pure potency and a real principle of the essence together with form. Matter is always considered in potency to all other forms of being. Form is considered to be the actual essence. Bearing in mind the Stagirite's identification of form and essence it is also proper to attribute the physical application of matter and form to Aristotle. Change was defined as the transition of a being from its potential to its actual state, matter being determined by form. In this sense it was used both by Aristotle and Aquinas and in this sense it is a purely physical theory because it makes no mention of potency as a principle of limit.

Metaphysics studies the same beings that physics considers but treats them from the viewpoint of being in general and as existing. This is the science within which St. Thomas makes his most fundamental application of the hylomorphic theory. Aristotle would make the same claim but the facts presented to us in the pages of the *corpus aristotelicum* do not bear him out. Considering Aristotelian philosophy in its whole context, it seems that the Stagirite used the hylomorphic theory solely with respect to change and the being of the categories, the being of immediate experience. Since these are the only applications found in his writings (and even they are found only in the logical and physical order), and since there is no distinction of essence and existence as a philosophical principle in Aristotle's philosophy, it would seem proper to state that he used the hylomorphic theory only in its application on the level of physical science. Even though his theory of individuation is indicative of an attempt to consider potency as a limiting principle, his failure to perceive the problem of individuality shows that his approach to reality was restricted to the experienced being of physics. Therefore the opinion of those who [1] hold that Aristotle considered hylomorphism as a metaphysical theory do not seem tenable in the light of the conclusions of the investigations pursued in this dissertation.

The theory of matter and form has its roots in change but fortunately is not restricted to, or dependent upon, the theories of physical science. If hylomorphism rested only upon physical science for its validity it would fall with the physical science of Aristotle and St. Thomas. Fortunately, however, hylomorphism has its metaphysical roots. The metaphysical validity of the theory rests solely on the reality of the potential and its capacity to limit act. Rejection of the physics of Aristotle and Aquinas is not a rejection of Thomistic metaphysics. Physics or natural science for St. Thomas was that part of philosophy which treats of things as capable of motion. St. Thomas used scientific theories of his own time as illustrations not as proofs. From this it cannot be inferred that his metaphysics rested upon physical science in our modern sense of the word. St. Thomas would say that to philosophize about science or even about such physical phenomena as the relation of the soul to the body demands a good knowledge of the empirical data related to these problems. And yet metaphysics is independent of all this. St. Thomas considered the hylomorphic theory as independent of scientific theories of his day on the nature of the elements. Hylomorphism is the result of a metaphysical analysis of experience. Prime matter is not the object of direct experience,

---

[1] H. Meyer, *The Philosophy of St. Thomas Aquinas*, p. 67.

no matter how refined modern laboratory equipment may be. Further, the hylomorphic theory is not an instrument of science from which new knowledge can be derived. It is rather a basic theory explaining in a general manner the genesis and motion and change that is characteristic of all things material. Furthermore, and perhaps more importantly in this day of modern scientific development, hylomorphism in presenting a universe of a gradation of forms, presents a world shot through with intelligibility, and this presentation is perhaps the most powerful single stimulus to modern scientific research. Nevertheless, the greatest single contribution of hylomorphism to science is to the science of metaphysics.

Hylomorphism is metaphysical when it is made subservient to the distinction between essence and existence, and this is what St. Thomas does. He considers essence and existence as a necessary pre-requisite of matter and form. If the distinction between essence and existence were denied, matter and form would be subsisting entities each with its own to be identical with its reality and the problem of the union of two entities which cannot make a unit would again present itself. The distinction of essence and existence is absolutely necessary to retain the unity of being. This has been the primary consideration given matter and form in this thesis because it is the primary instance of the use of the theory by St. Thomas. The application on the metaphysical level is more profound. It is the act of to be actuating the essence that confers unity of existence upon the elements of this essence which has been divided to explain change. The conferral of being is synonymous with the conferral of unity.

St. Thomas found his way to a universal hylomorphism, a metaphysical and not merely a physical use of the theory. He reasoned that it was possible to extend the hylomorphic way of thinking to all realms of being where the incomplete and imperfect may be considered as the underlying substrate in some manner completing and forming the actuality. His presentation makes it clear that the theory is essentially metaphysical. It enunciates the elements which bodies must possess in order to provide not only an intelligent account of matter and motion but also a rational description of finite existents. St. Thomas used hylomorphism metaphysically in this manner to explain how many distinctly individual beings retain their individuality in the presence of the multitude of their class. The theory therefore is descriptive of the structure of reality and explanatory of the problems of being, for together with essence and existence it provides a solution to both individuality and individuation.

Since the existence of beings precedes their change, discussion of the structure of being precedes the explanation of change in being. From this it is to be inferred that hylomorphism is primarily a metaphysical theory because as a phase of the distinction of essence and existence, it attempts to account for the individual existence of all things considered as existing. Furthermore, it does not seem that matter and form may even be used as an argument for change without the distinction of essence and existence in a prior metaphysical application. Logic demands that the metaphysical precede the physical applications. In this sense, therefore, matter and form become a contribution to and an additional justification of the existential position.

The existentialist interpretation of matter and form which refers the composition of essence to the prior distinction of essence and existence makes hylomorphism itself metaphysical. Aristotle, as well as most other ancient and mediaeval essentialistic philosophers, had a theory of matter and form but their failure to consider the theory in terms of the existential significance of being limited the logical use of hylomorphism to the physical application to the problems of matter and motion. Aristotle's essentialism for instance creates some difficulty because of its exaltation of matter as the principle of individuation in a philosophy which lacks any act of to be assuring the unity of the being. In short, matter and form on the physical level demand the metaphysical distinction of essence and existence because there can be no granting of a form of existence if first there has not been a granting of existence itself. It is the whole thing which exists,[2] the act of existence by which a substance exists is received by that substance through its form. It is the act of existence, not the form, which designates a " thing " a " being." [3] Considered metaphysically, matter and form

---

[2] *C. G.*, II, 54.   [3] *Ibid.*

is the most powerful argument for the participation theory. Form becomes the medium of participation and this dissertation becomes an argument for the real distinction of essence and existence in finite being simply because the division of an essence into matter and form necessarily demands a previous bestowal upon that essence of the act of existence which is but a transcendental aspect of its unity.

2.   Regarding the Problem of Being

Using the historical method we have traced in this dissertation the development of the theory of matter and form from its origins in early Greek philosophy of nature, to its refinement in the philosophies of Plato and Aristotle, and finally to its most noble application in the Christian metaphysics of St. Thomas Aquinas. The historical study of the progressive refinement of these notions has shown how material and formal causality take on an additional significance as they are more intimately related to a notion of being considered as the exercise of the act of existence. The study of the relationship of material and formal causality to the notion of being gives rise to the following conclusions.

1.   Thomistic metaphysics is existential because of its unique notion of being and the transcendentally analogous manner of thinking by which it is known. Being as act of existence is the focal point of every phase of St. Thomas' philosophy and *a fortiori* of material and formal causes as treated in this dissertation.

2.   This notion of being as act of existence is uniquely Thomistic. It is neither Platonic nor Aristotelian but a synthesis of both made in the light of an original intuition. For both Plato and Aristotle being is to be equated with form. Their corresponding theories of causality reflect, especially in the case of Aristotle, that being is a formal cause identical with the essence of a thing and that the other causes are causes to the precise extent that they contribute to the *form* of being. In contrast to this essentialism in which formal cause predominates, St. Thomas' theory of cause indicates that a thing is a cause precisely as it makes a contribution to existence. He therefore gives special prominence to the role of efficient and final causes.

3. The problem of reality is answered in terms of the individuality of being by means of a notion of being that is act of existence, and in terms of the individuation of being by material and formal causality that is related to the act of existence as potency to act. The problem of the one and the many in the order of existence (Individuality) is solved by this notion of being in which essence and existence are distinct. Further, the division of essence into matter and form as an explanation of change and individuation is made meaningful in the light of the prior distinction. Matter and form become truly metaphysical because, as potential to act of existence, they become explanatory aspects of the distinction of essence and existence.

We have not considered the whole philosophical problem of material being. That is the task of other sciences, both philosophical and natural. Our investigation has been restricted to the problem of the one and the many in the order of specific perfection (problem of individuation) as this problem is an aspect of the one and the many in the order of existence (problem of individuality). Our approach has been metaphysical, consisting of a consideration of the operation of various aspects of causality. Our aim has been specific, consisting of an evaluation of the contribution of the solution of the problem of the one and the many in terms of the causality of the form in Aristotelian philosophy on the one hand, and in terms of the causality of the Thomistic act of existence on the other. The effort has been to determine and evaluate the contribution of the predominant causality of each to the fundamental conception of the structure of being. Our conclusion is that hylomorphism provides an accurate description of the structure of essence in the field of metaphysics and an adequate explanation of changing being in the field of physics only when material and formal causality are viewed in a potential relationship to the act of existence. The metaphysical primacy of hylomorphism is a conclusion of this dissertation because it is a conclusion of the existential philosophy of St. Thomas Aquinas.

The Angelic Doctor's philosophy is a synthesis that is historic because it is original. His work is now a matter of history. The present work may not make history but it deals with historical fact.

simply because it treats of a philosophy which is concerned with being at the level of concrete essences. St. Thomas claims a unique position in the history of philosophy as the Christian philosopher of existence. Like his predecessor Aristotle, he wrestled with the ubiquitous problem of being. In this he was not unique. The originality of his endeavor and the significance of his achievement lay in his approach to the problem where it first presents itself to the philosopher, namely on the level of the existence of the finite beings of sensitive and intellectual experience. Plato concerned himself with the contribution of the ideal to the real; Aristotle with the contribution of form to material reality; St. Thomas with the contribution of act of existence to reality. He allowed neither of his predecessors to lead him astray in his attempt to account for the reality of *esse* in the heart of participated and contingent beings. From the being of experience in five tremendous strides (change, efficiency, contingency, participation and finality), St. Thomas advanced to the source of all existence. He explained individual existence in terms of the existence of God. The answer to the problem of existence is sought and found in the existence of Him Whose Essence It is To Be, the creative and conservative act of an almighty and omniscient God by Whom existence is communicated. The problem of existence is not resolved in the abstract ideas of a Plato, nor in Aristotle's concepts of essences nor even in the intelligible forms but in actually existing beings; beings which fill the universe, establish the limits of philosophy, and make history by giving form to matter.

BIBLIOGRAPHY

PRIMARY SOURCES

Aquinas, Saint Thomas. *Opera Omnia.* 25 vols. Parma (Fiaccadori), 1852-
1873. Photographic reproduction, New York: Musurgia Publishers,
1948-1949.

————. *Opera Omnia.* 16 vols. (to date), ed. Leonine. Rome: Leonine
Commission, 1882-1948.

————. *Summa Contra Gentiles.* Rome: Leonine Commission, 1934.

————. *Quaestiones Disputatae.* 2 vols., ed. R. Spiazzi et al. Rome:
Marietti, 1954.

————. *Quaestiones Quodlibetales,* ed. R. Spiazzi. Rome: Marietti, 1949.

————. *Opuscula Philosophica,* ed. R. Spiazzi. Rome: Marietti, 1954.

————. *Opuscula Theologica.* 2 vols., ed. R. Verardo and R. Spiazzi. Rome:
Marietti, 1954.

————. *Expositio Super Librum De Causis,* ed. H. D. Saffrey. Fribourg-
Louvain: E. Nauwelaerts, 1954.

————. *In Aristotelis Librum De Anima Commentarium,* ed. A. M. Pirotta.
Rome: Marietti, 1948.

————. *In Aristotelis Libros De Sensu et Sensato, De Memoria et Remi-
niscentia Commentarium,* ed. R. Spiazzi. Rome: Marietti, 1949.

————. *In Aristotelis Libros Peri Hermeneias et Posterior Analyticorum
Expositio,* ed. R. Spiazzi. Rome: Marietti, 1955.

————. *In Decem Libros Ethicorum Aristotelis Ad Nicomachum Expositio,*
ed. R. Spiazzi. Rome: Marietti, 1949.

————. *In Aristotelis Libros De Coelo et Mundo, De Generatione et Cor-
ruptione, Meterorologicorum Expositio,* ed. R. Spiazzi. Rome:
Marietti, 1952.

————. *In Duodecim Libros Metaphysicorum Aristotelis Expositio,* ed.
Cathala-Spiazzi. Rome: Marietti, 1950.

————. *In Octo Libros Physicorum Aristotelia Expositio,* ed. P. M.
Maggiolo. Rome: Marietti, 1954.

————. *Scriptum Super Sententiis Magistri Petri Lombardi.* 4 vols., ed.
M. F. Moos. Paris: Lethielleux, 1947.

————. *Summa Theologiae.* 5 vols., ed. Ottowa, Ottowa: Studium Generale
Ordinis Praedicatorum, 1943.

————. *De Ente et Essentia,* ed. M.-D. Roland-Gosselin. Kain (Belgique):
Le Saulchoir, 1926.

————. *In Dionysium de divinis nominibus expositio,* ed. C. P. Pera.
Rome: Marietti, 1950.

45

————. *Expositio Super Librum Boethii De Trinitate,* ed. B. Decker. Leiden (Netherlands) : Brill, 1955.

————. *On Being and Essence,* trans. A. Maurer. Toronto: Pontifical Institute of Mediaeval Studies, 1949.

————. *The Division and Method of the Sciences.* Questions V and VI of his *Commentary on the "De Trinitate" of Boethius,* trans. A. Maurer. Toronto: Pontifical Institute of Mediaeval Studies, 1953.

Aristotle. *Opera Omnia.* 5 vols., ed. I. Bekker. Berlin: G. Reimer, 1831-1870. [Vols. 1, 2 Text, ed. I. Bekker; and Fragments, ed. V. Rose. Vol. 3 Renaissance Latin translations. Vol. 4 *Scholia,* ed. C. A. Brandis and H. Usener. Vol. 5 *Index Aristotelicus,* ed. H. Bonitz].

————. Aristotelis. *Opera Omnia,* Grace et Latine. 5 vols. Paris: Fermin-Didot et Sociis, 1848-1873.

————. *Aristotelis Metaphysica.* 2 vols. Bonn: Marcus, 1848-1849.

————. *Aristotle's Metaphysics.* A revised text with Introduction and Commentary. 2 vols., ed. W. D. Ross. Oxford: Clarendon Press, 1948.

————. *The Metaphysics.* With an English translation. 2nd ed. revised, 2 vols. (in *The Loeb Classical Library*), ed. H. Trendennick. Cambridge, Mass.: Harvard University Press, 1947.

————. *Aristotle's Physics.* A revised text with Introduction and Commentary, ed. W. D. Ross. Oxford: Clarendon Press, 1955.

————. *Aristotle's Prior and Posterior Analytics.* A revised text with Introduction and Commentary, ed. W. D. Ross. Oxford: Clarendon Press, 1949.

————. *The Works of Aristotle.* 12 vols., 2d ed., trans. W. D. Ross *et al.* Oxford: Clarendon Press, 1928.

————. *The Basic Works of Aristotle,* ed. R. McKeon. New York: Random House, 1941.

Diels, H. *Die Fragments der Vorsokratiker, Griechisch und Deutsch.* 3 vols. 5 ed. W. Kranz. Berlin: Weidmann, 1934-1937.

————. *Doxographie Graeci.* 2 ed. Berlin: Walter de Grytes et Soc., 1929.

Freeman, Kathleen. *Ancilla to the Pre-Socratic Philosophers.* A complete translation of the Fragments in *Diels, Fragmente der Vorsokratiker.* Oxford: Basil Blackwell, 1952.

Plato. *Platonis Dialogi graece et latine,* 8 vols., ed. I. Bekker. Berlin: Reimer, 1816-18.

————. *Platonis Opera.* 5 vols., ed. J. Burnet. Oxford: Clarendon Press, 1905-1910.

————. *The Dialogues of Plato.* 2 vols., trans. B. Jowett. New York: Random House, 1937.

————. *Plato's Theory of Knowledge.* The *Theaetetus* and *Sophist* of Plato translated with a running commentary by F. M. Cornford. London: Routledge and Kegan Paul, 1935.

————. *Plato's Cosmology.* The *Timaeus* of Plato translated with a running commentary by F. M. Cornford. London: Routledge and Kegan Paul, 1937.

———. *Plato and Parmenides*. Parmenides' *Way of Truth* and Plato's *Parmenides* translated with a running commentary by F. M. Cornford. London: Routledge and Kegan Paul, 1939.

SECONDARY SOURCES

A. Books

Albertus, Saint Albert the Great. *Opera Omnia.* 35 vols., ed. Borgnet. Paris: Vives, 1890-1899.

Allen, D. J. *The Philosophy of Aristotle.* New York: Oxford University Press, 1952.

Anderson, J. F. *The Bond of Being.* St. Louis, Mo.: Herder, 1949.

———. *The Cause of Being.* St. Louis, Mo.: Herder, 1952.

———. *The Metaphysics of St. Thomas Aquinas.* Chicago: Regnery, 1953.

Assenmacher, J. *Die Geschichte des Individuationsprinzips in Der Scholastik.* Leipzig: F. Meiner, 1926.

Ast, F. *Lexicon Platonicum.* Berlin: Bardsdorf, 1908.

Averroes. *Tahafut Al-Tahafut* (*The Incoherence of the Incoherence*), 2 vols., trans. with Introduction and Notes by S. Van Den Bergh. Oxford: at the University Press: Trustees of E. J. W. Gibb Memorial, 1954.

Avicebron. *Avicebrolis Fons Vitae,* ed. C. Baeumker. Münster: *Beiträge zur Geschichte der Philosophie des Mittelalters,* Band I, Heft 2, 1892.

Baeumker, C. *Das Problem der Materie in der Griechischen Philosophie.* Münster: Aschendorffschen, 1890.

Barrett, W. *Aristotle's Analysis of Movement: Its Significance for Its Time.* New York: Columbia University Press, 1938.

Balthasar, N. *La Méthode en Metaphysique.* Louvain: Institute of Higher Studies, 1943.

Banez, D. *Commentarios ineditos a la Prima secundae de Santo Tomás.* 2 vols. Edicion preparada por el R. P. Mtro. Vincente Beltram de Heredis. Madrid, 1942.

———. *Commentarios ineditos a la tercera parte de Santo Tomas.* 2 vols. Madrid, 1951.

Bannan, J. F. "Exemplar Causality in the Philosophy of Saint Thomas." Unpublished M. A. dissertation, School of Philosophy. The Catholic University of America. Washington, D. C., 1950.

Bergson, H. *Creative Evolution,* trans. A. Mitchell. (Reprint). London: Macmillan, 1954.

———. *The Creative Mind,* trans. M. Andison. (Reprint). New York: Philosophical Library, 1946.

Boethius. *The Tractates and the Consolation of Philosophy* (in *The Loeb*

Classical Library), trans. H. F. Stewart and E. K. Rand. Cambridge, Mass.: Harvard University Press, 1953.

Bonaventure, Saint. *Opera Omnia*. 10 vols. Quaracchi, 1892-1902.

Bonitz, H. *Index Aristotelicus* (in Prussian Academy *Aristotelis Opera*, Vol. V.). Berlin: Reimer, 1870.

Bourke, V. *Thomistic Bibliography*. St. Louis, Mo.: *The Modern Schoolman Supplement,* 1945.

Boyer, C. *Cursus Philosophicus*. 2 vols. Brugis (Belgium): Desclée de Brouwer, 1954.

Brehier, E. *Histoire de la Philosophie*. Vols. I and II. Paris: Alcan, 1926.

Brentano, F. *Aristotles Lehre vom Ursprung des Menschlichen Geistes*. Leipzig: Veit and Co., 1911.

Buckley, J. *Man's Last End*. St. Louis: Herder, 1949.

Burnet, J. *Early Greek Philosophy*. 4th ed. London: Macmillan, 1930.

Burtt, E. A. (ed.). *The English Philosophers from Bacon to Mill*. (in *The Modern Library*). New York: Random House, 1939.

————. *The Metaphysical Foundations of Modern Science*, rev. ed. Garden City, N. Y.: Doubleday Anchor Books, 1954.

Cajetan, Thomas de Vio. *In De Ente et Essentia D. Thomae Aquinatis Commentaria*, ed. M.-H. Laurent. Turin: Marietti, 1934.

Cherniss, H. *Aristotle's Criticism of Plato and the Academy*. Baltimore: The Johns Hopkins Press, 1944.

————. *Aristotle's Criticism of Pre-Socratic Philosophy*. Baltimore, Md.: The Johns Hopkins Press, 1935.

Coffey, P. *Ontology*. (reprint). New York: Peter Smith, 1938.

————. *The Science of Logic*. (reprint). New York: Peter Smith, 1938.

Collins, J. *A History of Modern European History*. Milwaukee: Bruce, 1954.

————. *The Thomistic Philosophy of the Angels*. Washington: The Catholic University of America Press, 1947.

Collins, R. J. "The Metaphysical Basis of Finality in St. Thomas." Unpublished Ph. D. dissertation, School of Philosophy, The Catholic University of America, 1947.

Cook, E. M. "The Transcendental Character of the Notion of Efficiency in the Metaphysics of St. Thomas." Unpublished M. A. dissertation, School of Philosophy, The Catholic University of America, 1956.

Copleston, F. C. *Aquinas*. Baltimore, Penguin Books, 1955.

————. *A History of Philosophy*. 3 vols. Westminster, Md.: Newman, 1953.

Dampier, W. C. *A History of Science*. New York: Macmillan, 1929.

Davitt, T. *The Nature of Law*. St. Louis: Herder, 1953.

Deferrari, R. J. and Barry, Sister M. I. *A Lexicon of St. Thomas Aquinas*. Washington: The Catholic University of America Press, 1948.

De Finance, A. *Être et Agir dans la philosophie de S. Thomas*. Paris: Beauschesne, 1945.

Descartes, R. *The Philosophical Works of Descartes*, trans. E. Haldane and G. Ross (reprint of 1938 ed.). New York: Dover Publications, 1955.

De Raeymaeker, L. *Introduction to Philosophy*, trans. H. MacNeill. New York: Wagner, 1948.

——. *The Philosophy of Being*, trans. E. Ziegelmeyer. St. Louis: Herder, 1954.

De Regnon, T. *La Metaphysique des Causes*. Paris: Victor Retaux, 1906.

Descoqs, P. *Essai Critique sur l'Hylemorphisme*. Paris: Beachesne, 1924.

De Wulf, M. *Philosophy and Civilization in the Middle Ages*. (reprint of 1929 ed). New York: Dover Publications, 1953.

Duhem, P. *Le Systeme du monde. Histoire des doctrines cosmologiques de Platon a Copernic.* (reprint). Paris: Hermann et Cie, 1954.

Dulles, A., Demske, J., O'Connell, R. *Introductory Metaphysics*. New York: Sheed and Ward, 1955.

Fabre, C. *La nozione metafisica di partecipazione*. 2d ed. Turin: Internezionile, 1950.

Farrington, B. *Greek Science*. (reprint of 1944-1949 ed.). Baltimore: Penguin, 1953.

Ferm, V. (ed.). *A History of Philosophical Systems*. New York: Philosophical Library, 1950.

Forest, A. *La structure metaphysique du concret selon Saint Thomas d'Aquin*. Paris: Vrin, 1931.

Frank, P. *Philosophy of Science*. Englewood Cliffs, N. J.: Prentice-Hall, 1957.

Galileo Galilei. *Dialogues concerning Two New Sciences*, trans. H. Crew and A. de Salvio. (reprint of 1914 ed.). New York: Dover Publications, n. d.

Garrigou-Lagrange, R. *God His Existence and His Nature*. 2 vols. St. Louis: Herder, 1934.

——. *Le Sens Commun*. Paris: Desclee de Brouwer, 1934.

——. *The One God*, trans. B. Rose. St. Louis: Herder, 1943.

——. *Reality*, trans. P. Cummins. St. Louis: Herder, 1953.

Geiger, L.-B. *La Participation dans la Philosophie de S. Thomas d'Aquin*. 2d ed. Paris: Vrin, 1953.

Gerrity, B. *The Theory of Matter and Form and the Theory of Knowledge*. Washington: The Catholic University of America Press, 1936.

Gilson, E. *Introduction a d'Étude de Saint Augustin*. Paris: Vrin, 1949.

——. *Jean Duns Scot*. Paris: Vrin, 1952.

——. *L'Être et L'Essence*. Paris: Vrin, 1948.

——. *Realisme Thomiste et Critique de la Connaissance*. Paris: Vrin, 1947.

——. *La Philosophie de S. Bonaventure*, 2d. ed. Paris: Vrin, 1943.

——. *Le Thomisme*. 5th ed. Paris: Vrin, 1947.

——. *The Christian Philosophy of St. Thomas Aquinas*. With a Catalogue of St. Thomas' Works by I. T. Eschmann, trans. L. K. Shook. New York: Random House, 1956.

———. *History of Christian Philosophy in the Middle Ages.* New York: Random House, 1957.

———. *The Spirit of Mediaeval Philosophy,* trans. A. H. C. Downes. New York: Scribner's, 1940.

———. *Being and Some Philosophers.* 2d ed. Toronto: Pontifical Institute of Mediaeval Studies, 1952.

———. *Reason and Revelation in the Middle Ages.* New York: Scribner's, 1954.

———. *God and Philosophy.* New Haven, Conn.: Yale University Press, 1941.

———. *Painting and Reality.* New York: Pantheon Books, 1955.

———. *The Unity of Philosophical Experience.* New York: Scribner's, 1954.

Goheen, J. *The Problem of Matter and Form in the " De Ente et Essentia " of Thomas Aquinas.* Cambridge, Mass.: Harvard University Press, 1940.

Grabmann, M. *Thomas Aquinas: His Personality and Thought,* trans. V. Michel. New York: Longmans, Green, 1928.

Gredt, J. *Elementa Philosophiae.* 2 vols., 8th ed. Fribourg: Herder, 1953.

Hamelin, O. *Le Système d'Aristote.* Paris: L. Robin, 1920.

Harper, T. *The Metaphysics of the School* (reprint). New York: Peter Smith, 1940.

Hart, C. A. *Metaphysics for the Many. A Thomistic Inquiry into the Act of Existing.* (Privately circulated edition of text soon to be published). Washington, D. C.: by the author, 1957.

Hausmann, E. and Slack, E. *Physics.* 3rd ed. New York: Van Nostrand, 1948.

Hawkins, D. J. B. *Being and Becoming.* London: Sheed and Ward, 1954.

———. *Causality and Implication.* New York: Sheed and Ward, 1937.

Hegel, G. W. F. *A Philosophy of History,* trans. J. Dibree. (reprint). New York: Dover Publications, 1956.

Henle, R. J. *Method in Metaphysics.* Milwaukee: Marquette University Press, 1951.

———. *Saint Thomas and Platonism.* The Hague: Nijhoff, 1956.

Hoenan, P. *Cosmologia.* 4th ed. rev. Rome: Gregorian University, 1955.

———. *De Origine Formae Materialis.* Rome: Gregorian University, 1951.

———. *Reality and Judgment According to St. Thomas,* trans. H. F. Tiblier. Chicago: Regnery, 1952.

Hugon, R. P. *Les Vinqt-Quatre Theses Thomiste.* Paris: Pequin, 1926.

Jaeger, W. *Aristotle.* 2d ed., trans R. Robinson. Oxford: Clarendon Press, 1948.

Jesuit Philosophical Association: Papers of the Fourteenth Annual Convention, *Hylomorphism and Contemporary Physics.* Presented by

J. Wulftange and M. Greene. (Privately circulated). Woodstock, Md.: Woodstock College Press, 1952.

John of St. Thomas. *Cursus Philosophicus Thomisticus.* 3 vols., ed. B. Reiser. Rome: Marietti, 1948.

Jolivet, R. *La Notion de Substance.* Paris: Beauchesne, 1929.

Jugnet, L. *La Pensée de Saint Thomas D'Aquin.* Paris: Bordas, 1949.

Kant, E. *Critique of Pure Reason,* trans. N. K. Smith. London: Macmillan, 1953.

Kirk, C. S. *Heraclitus, the Cosmic Fragments.* Cambridge: The University Press, 1954.

Klubertanz, G. P. *Introduction to the Philosophy of Being.* New York: Appleton-Century-Crofts, 1955.

————. *The Philosophy of Human Nature.* New York: Appleton-Century-Crofts, 1953.

Koren, H. J. *An Introduction to the Science of Metaphysics.* St. Louis: Herder, 1955.

Krempel, A. *La doctrine de la relation chez S. Thomas.* Paris: Vrin, 1952.

Lalande, A. *Vocabulaire Technique et Critique de la Philosophie.* 7th ed. rev. Paris: Presses Universitaires de France, 1956.

Lang, A. *Das Kausalproblem.* 2 vols. Köln: J. P. Bochem, 1904.

Leibnitz. *The Monadology.* And Other Philosophical Writings. (reprint of 1898 ed), trans. R. Latta. London: Oxford University Press, 1951.

Lewis, C. and Snort, C. *Latin Dictionary.* New York: American Book Co., 1907.

Liddell, H. G. and Scott, R. *A Greek-English Lexicon.* New edition revised and augmented by H. S. Jones and R. McKenzie (reprint of 9th ed. of 1940). Oxford: Clarendon Press, 1953.

Little, A. *The Platonic Heritage of Thomism.* Dublin: Golden Eagle Books, 1949.

Lodge, R. C. *The Philosophy of Plato.* London: Routledge and Kegan Paul, 1956.

Lottin, O. *Psychologie et Morale aux XIIe et XIIIe Siècles.* 6 vols. Gimbloux (Belgique): J. Ducolot, 1947-1954.

Lowyck, E. *Substantiele Verandering en Hylemorphisme.* Louvain: Institute of Higher Studies, 1948.

Maimonides, Moses. *The Guide for the Perplexed,* trans. M. Friedländer (reprint of 2d revised ed. of Routledge, Kegan Paul). New York: Dover Publications, 1956.

Manser, G. M. *Das Wesen Des Thomismus.* Freiburg (Schweiz): Paulusverlag, 1949.

Mansion, A. *Introduction à la Physique Aristotelicienne.* Paris: Vrin, 1956.

Mansion, S. *Le Jugement D'Existence chez Aristote.* Paris: Desclée De Brouwer, 1944.

Maquart, F.-X. *Elementa Philosophiae.* 3 vols. Paris: Blot, 1938.

Marechal, J. *Le Point de Depart de la Metaphysique.* Cahier V. Paris: Desclee De Brouwer, 1949.

Maritain, J. *An Essay on Christian Philosophy.* New York: Philosophical Library, 1955.

――――. *Approaches to God,* trans. P. O. Reilly. New York: Harper, 1954.

――――. *A Preface to Metaphysics.* New York: Sheed and Ward, 1948.

――――. *Art and Scholasticism,* trans. J. F. Scanlon. New York: Scribner's, 1954.

――――. *Creative Intuition in Art and Poetry.* New York: Pantheon, 1953.

――――. *Existence and the Existent,* trans. L. Galantiere and G. B. Phelan. New York: Pantheon, 1948.

――――. *Introduction to Philosophy,* trans. E. I. Watkin. New York: Sheed and Ward, n. d.

――――. *Les Degrés du Savoir.* 5th ed. rev. Paris: Desclée de Brouwer, 1946.

――――. *The Philosophy of Nature.* New York: Philosophical Library, 1951.

――――. *The Range of Reason.* New York: Scribner's, 1953.

――――. *Science and Wisdom,* trans. B. Wall. New York: Scribner's, 1940.

Marling, J. *The Order of Nature in the Philosophy of St. Thomas.* Washington: The Catholic University of America Press, 1934.

Martin, W. O. *The Order and Integration of Knowledge.* Ann Arbor, Mich.: University of Michigan Press, 1957.

Mattiussi, G. *Les points fondamentaux de la philosophie thomiste,* trans. J. Levillain. Rome: Marietti, 1926.

McCall, R. *The Reality of Substance.* Washington: The Catholic University of America Press, 1956.

McWilliams, J. A. *Physics and Philosophy.* A Study of St. Thomas' Commentary on the Eight Books of Aristotle's Physics. Vol. 2 of Philosophical Studies of the American Catholic Philosophical Association. Washington: By the Association, 1945.

――――. (ed.). *Progress in Philosophy.* Philosophical Studies in Honor of Reverend Doctor Charles A. Hart. Milwaukee: Bruce, 1955.

Meehan, F. *Efficient Causality in Aristotle and St. Thomas.* Washington: The Catholic University of America Press, 1940.

――――. "The Thomistic Concept of the Possible, the Potential and the Actual." Unpublished M. A. dissertation. School of Philosophy, The Catholic University of America, 1937.

Meyer, H. *The Philosophy of St. Thomas Aquinas,* trans. E. Eckhoff. St. Louis: Herder, 1944.

Michelitsch, A. *Illustrierte Geschichte der Philosophie.* Graz: Styria, 1933.

Nahm, M. C. *Selections from Early Greek Philosophy.* 2d ed. New York: Crofts, 1940.

O'Neill, J. *Cosmology*. New York: Longmans, Green, 1923.

Owens, J. *The Doctrine of Being in the Aristotelian Metaphysics*. Toronto: Pontifical Institute of Mediaeval Studies, 1951.

———. *St. Thomas and the Future of Metaphysics*. Milwaukee: ˋMarquette University Press, 1957.

Pegis, A. *St. Thomas and the Greeks*. Milwaukee: Marquette University Press, 1939.

Phelan, G. B. *St. Thomas and Analogy*. Milwaukee: Marquette University Press, 1941.

Philippe, M. D. *Initiation a la Philosophie D'Aristote*. Paris: La Colombe, 1956.

Phillips, R. P. *Modern Thomistic Philosophy*. 2 vols. Westminster, Md.: Newman, 1948.

Plotinus. *The Enneads*, trans. S. MacKenna. 2d ed. rev. by B. S. Page. London: Faber and Faber, 1956.

Proceedings of the American Catholic Philosophical Association. Vol XXI, "Philosophy of Being," ed. C. A. Hart. Washington: By the Association, 1946.

Renard, H. *The Philosophy of Being*. Milwaukee: Bruce, 1946.

———. *The Philosophy of God*. Milwaukee: Bruce, 1951.

———. *The Philosophy of Man*. Milwaukee: Bruce, 1948.

Renoirte, F. *Cosmology*, trans. J. Coffey. New York: Wagner, 1950.

Ritter, C. *The Essence of Plato's Philosophy*, trans. A. Alles. New York: The Dial Press, 1933.

Robin, L. *Aristote*. Paris: Presses Universitaires de France, 1944.

———. *Greek Thought and the Origins of the Scientific Spirit*, trans. N. R. Dobie. London: Kegan Paul, 1928.

Rosenberg, J. "The Principle of Individuation. A Comparative Study of St. Thomas, Suarez, Scotus." Unpublished Ph. D. dissertation, School of Philosophy, The Catholic University of America, 1950.

Ross, D. *Aristotle*. 5th ed. London: Methuen, 1953.

———. *Plato's Theory of Ideas*. 2d ed. Oxford: Clarendon Press, 1953.

Runner, H. E. *The Development of Aristotle Illustrated from the Earliest Books of the Physics*. Amsterdam: Free University of Amsterdam, 1951.

Ryan, J. K. (ed.). *Philosophical Studies in Honor of the Very Reverend Ignatius Smith, O. P.* Westminster, Md.: Newman, 1952.

Schütz, L. *Thomas-Lexikon* (reprint). New York: Ungar, 1957.

Scotus, John Duns. *Opera Omnia*. 26 vols., 2d ed. Paris, Vives, 1891-1895.

Singer, C., et al. *A History of Technology*. Vols. I and II. Oxford: Clarendon Press, 1954.

Smeets, A. *Act en Potencie in de Metaphysics van Aristoteles* (avec une résumé en français). Louvain: University of Louvain, 1952.

Smith, V. E. *The Philosophical Frontiers of Physics*. Washington: The Catholic University of America Press, 1947.

————. *Philosophical Physics*. New York: Harper, 1950.

Smolko, J. F. "The Notion of Intrinsic Principles in the Metaphysics of St. Thomas." Unpublished M. A. dissertation. School of Philosophy, The Catholic University of America, 1953.

Sparks, T. M. *De Divisione Causae Exemplaris Apud S. Thomam*. Somerset, Ohio: The Rosary Press, 1936.

Suarez, F. *Opera Omnia*. 32 vols. Paris: Vives, 1856-1877.

Sylvestris, Franciscus de (Ferrariensis). *Commentaria in Libros Quatuor Contra Gentiles S. Thomas de Aquino*. 4 vols., ed. J. Sestilli. Rome: Orphanotrophium a S. Hieronymo Aemeliani, 1897-1900.

Taylor, A. E. *Aristotle* (reprint of revised edition of 1919). New York: Dover Publications, 1955.

————. *Aristotle on his Predecessors*. Being the First Book of his Metaphysics. Chicago: Open Court, 1907.

————. *Plato, the Man and His Work* (reprint of 6th ed.). London: Methuen, 1952.

Trever, A. A. *History of Ancient Civilization*. 2 vols. New York: Harcourt, Brace, 1936.

Ueberweg, F. and Praechter, K. *Die Philosophie des Altertum*. Berlin: Mittler, 1926.

Van Laer, H. *Philosophico-Scientific Problems*, trans. H. Koren. Pittsburgh, Pa.: Duquesne University Press, 1953.

Van Melsen, A. O. *From Atomos to Atom*, trans. H. Koren. Pittsburgh, Pa.: Duquesne University Press, 1952.

————. *The Philosophy of Nature*. Pittsburgh, Pa.: Duquesne University Press, 1954.

Van Steenberghen, F. *Aristotle in the West*, trans. L. Johnson. Louvain: E. Nauwelaerts, 1955.

————. *Ontology*, trans M. Flynn. New York: Wagner, 1952.

————. *The Philosophical Movement in the Thirteenth Century*. London: Nelson, 1955.

Wuellner, B. *Summary of Scholastic Principles*. Chicago: Loyola University Press, 1956.

Zeller, E. *Aristotle and the Earlier Paripatetics*, trans. B. Costelloe and J. Muirhead. London: Longmans, Green, 1879.

B. *Selected Articles*

Anderson, J. Review of *The Doctrine of Being in the Aristotelian Metaphysics*, by J. Owens, *New Scholasticism*, XXVI (1952), pp. 229-238.

Annice, Sister M. "Historical Sketch of the Theory of Participation," *New Scholasticism*, XXVI (1952), pp. 47-79.

Balz, A. G. A . "Prime Matter and Physical Science," *Proceedings and Addresses of the American Philosophical Association*, XXIX (1955-1956), pp. 5-25.

Berto, V. A. "Sur la composition d'acte et de puissance dans les creatures d'après S. Thomas," *Revue de Philosophie*, XXXIX (1939), pp. 106-121.

Bobik, J. "Dimensions in the Individuation of Bodily Substances," *Philosophical Studies* (Maynooth), IV (1954), pp. 60-79.

Bremond, A. "Le synthèse thomiste de l'Acte et de l'Idée," *Gregorianum*, XII (1931), pp. 267-283.

Clark, W. W. "The Limitation of Act by Potency," *New Scholasticism*, XXVI (1952), pp. 167-194.

De Lacy, P. H. "The Problem of Causation in Plato's Philosophy," *Classical Philology*, XXXIV (1939), pp. 97-115.

De Saint-Maurice, B. "Existential Import in the Philosophy of Duns Scotus," *Franciscan Studies*, IX (1949), pp. 274-313.

Dubarle, D. "La Causalité dans la philosophie d'Aristote," in *Recherches de Philosophie* 1: Histoire de la Philosophie et Metaphysique. Paris: Desclée de Brouwer, 1955.

Geny, P. "Le Probleme Metaphysique de la Limitation de l'Acte," *Revue de Philosophie* (1919), pp. 129-156.

Gredt, J. "Doctrina thomistica de potentia et actu . . . ," *Acta Ponto Academiae Romanae S. Thomae*, I (1935), pp. 33-49.

Hamelin, O. "La Nature et le Mouvement d'Après Aristote," *Revue Philosophique*, LXXXVII (1919), pp. 353-368.

Hart, C. A. "Participation and the Thomistic Five Ways," *New Scholasticism*, XXVI (1952), pp. 207-282.

———. "Twenty-Five Years of Thomism," *New Scholasticism*, XXV (1951), pp. 3-45.

Kane, W. "Abstraction and the Distinction of the Sciences," *Thomist*, XVI (1954), pp. 43-69.

Mandonnet, P. "Les Premières disputes sur la distinction réelé entre l'essence et l'existence" *Revue Thomiste*, XVIII (1910), pp. 741-765.

Maquart, F. X. "Aristotle n'a-t-il affirme qu'une distinction logique entre l'essence et l'existence," *Revue Thomiste*, XXVI (1926), pp. 62-72.

Maurer, A. "Form and Essence in the Philosophy of St. Thomas," *Mediaeval Studies*, XII (1951), pp. 165-176.

McMullen, E. "Hylemorphism and Temporality," *Philosophical Studies* (Maynooth), VI (1956), pp. 126-138.

Michel, A. "Essence," *Dictionnaire Theologie Catholique*, t. V, I partie, ccl. 831-850.

Michon, R. "L'Acte et la puissance dans la synthèse thomiste," *Revue de Philosophie*, XXVIII (1928), pp. 56-87.

Miller, R. G. "The Empirical Dilemma: Either Metaphysics or Nonsense," *Proceedings of the American Catholic Philosophical Association*, XXIX (1955), pp. 151-176.

O'Donoghue, D. "Aristotle's Doctrine of 'The Underlying Matter'—A

Study of the First Book of the Physics," *Philosophical Studies* (Maynooth), III (1953), pp. 16-39.

Owens, J. "An Aristotelian Text Related to the Distinction of Being and Essence," *Proceedings of the American Catholic Philosophical Association*, XXI (1946), pp. 165-172.

————. "Our Knowledge of Nature," *Proceedings of the American Catholic Philosophical Association*, XXIX (1955), pp. 63-86.

Peters, J. A. J. "Matters and Form in Metaphysics," *New Scholasticism*, XXXI (1957), pp. 447-483.

Phelan, G. B. "The Existentialism of St. Thomas," *Proceedings of the American Catholic Philosophical Association*, XXI (1946), pp. 25-40.

————. "The Being of Creatures: St. Thomas' Solution of the Dilemma of Parmenides and Heraclitus," *Proceedings of the American Catholic Philosophical Association*, XXXI (1957), pp. 118-125.

Robin, L. "Sur la conception aristotelicienne de la causalité," *Archiv fur Geschichte der Philosophie*, XXIII (1910), pp. 1-28; 184-210.

Seiler, J. "Physics and the Scholastic Theory of Matter and Form," *Crosscurrents*, IV (1954), pp. 165-177.